LifeLaunch

A Passionate Guide to the Rest of Your Life

Frederic M. Hudson and Pamela D. McLean

Fourth Edition, revised, 2006

ISBN 13: 978-1-884433-84-9
ISBN 10: 1-884433-84-7
Library of Congress: 94-096041

Price: $24.95

The Hudson Institute Press
350 S. Hope Ave., Suite A210
Santa Barbara, CA 93105
Phone: 805-682-3883
Fax: 805-569-0025
www.hudsoninstitute.com

Copyright 1995
Second Edition, Revised, 1996
Third Edition, Revised, 2000
Fourth Edition, 2001
Fourth Edition, Revised, 2006

Book & cover design by Nanette Boyer
Book editor, Donna Bushnell
Cover Illustration, Michelle Shapiro

This book is dedicated
to our children
Christopher, Michael & Charlie
For the Adventures Ahead!

Table of Contents

Section I: Prepare to Journey Ahead

Section II: Consult your Compass, Follow these Maps

Section III: Launch the Next Chapter of your Life

Section IV: Resources

About the Authors

Frederic M. Hudson an educator, writer, and trainer, is a recognized expert in adult change. He is widely respected for his contributions to the fields of adult development, career transition planning and human and organizational development.

As a Rockefeller and Danforth Fellow, he earned his doctorate at Columbia University in New York, and taught at Colby College and the University of San Francisco. From 1974 through 1986 he was the founding president of The Fielding Institute, a leading adult learning system and professional graduate school for advanced study in organizational development and psychology.

In 1987 he founded The Hudson Institute of Santa Barbara—a training center focused on coaching and renewal in the workplace and for the individual. Its central theme is to train adults as masters of change, with proactive lives and careers.

Dr. Hudson was named "Executive Coach of the Year" by AT&T, "The Best Seminar Leader We've Ever Had" by 3M, and "Life/Work Balance Coach" by Harley-Davidson. He has been called "Dr. Midlife" by the *Los Angeles Times*, and "the Dr. Spock of the Adult Years" by a reviewer of his latest book, *The Adult Years: Mastering the Art of Self-Renewal,* which another reviewer hailed as "the *Passages* of the 2000's…the most compelling book ever written on personal transition and transformation."

Pamela D. McLean, whose doctoral research was on how adult women plan their lives, is a clinical psychologist in private practice in Santa Barbara, California. She has served on the adjunct faculties of the University of North Dakota, Santa Barbara Community College, Antioch University, and The Hudson Institute. She is especially interested in female development, family rituals, and parenting issues. Drs. McLean and Hudson are married and the parents of three boys.

The authors thank Nanette Boyer for her unique creativity and ingenuity in the design of the book as well as this revised book cover. Also, our thanks are extended to the late Donna Bushnell for her expert eyes and judgements in the editing of the original text. Our thanks to Billy Escue, a coach and entrepreneur who encouraged this latest revision of the book and who has helped enormously in "spreading the word" about this book.

PREFACE

My Wake-up Call— Lessons Learned

by Frederic M. Hudson

My life course was shaped indelibly by a powerful event in my childhood that taught me a great deal about LifeLaunching. Although I have shared this story on many occasions, I repeat it here because it vividly represents the message and purpose of this book: *have a vision, get a plan, and stay on course.*

On August 23, 1943, when I was nine years old, I awakened in silent terror. I was unable to move any part of my body except my eyes. My muscles seemed frozen, and my voice was silenced. Although I had gone to bed as a walking, talking, wiggling boy, I woke up the next day paralyzed with polio. Neither my legs nor my arms would respond to my desperate efforts to move, and my neck and jaw were as rigid as rocks. Breathing was panicked and pain was everywhere. In the 1940s, polio was a dreaded epidemic of unidentified origin for which there was no means of prevention, and no real medical treatment. Many who contracted it died; others went through life in braces and wheelchairs.

The next thing I remember was lying on the back seat of my parents' old automobile as they drove me thirty miles from my home in upstate New York to a hospital in Syracuse. That journey was unbelievably painful. I was sicker than I had ever felt in my life. I felt a helplessness and fear never experienced before. "What will happen to me?" I pondered. "Am I going to die? Will I ever see my family again? It isn't fair. . . ." That day remains vivid in my mind, like a screeching siren I couldn't turn off.

At the hospital, they placed me on a very hard bed—with no pillow, in a quarantined ward. I spent my waking moments staring upward at the ceiling—my only option—and feeling totally helpless. The main treatment I received were "Sister Kenny" hot packs administered frequently throughout the day and night, so hot that they scorched my body and smelled like wet, burnt wool—a smell branded to my mind.

A wise nurse named Susan spent lots of time with me. Quiet and caring, she visited me frequently and told me many things. Her main message went like this: "Your future, Frederic, is hidden on the ceiling, and you are the only one who can find it. Look for what you will be doing as you grow up. It's all up there. Will you be a track star, a tennis player, a scientist? Will you be going on trips to faraway places? Will you be going to summer camps and swimming? Will you go to college and become someone special? Will you marry and have a family? Frederic, all you have to do is to study the ceiling. When you see your future, it will start to happen!"

That's all she ever talked about—my future. I spent hours and then days and months searching for snap-shots of my future in the maze on that dirty ceiling above my immobile body. There were many designs discernible there, with cracks in the plaster and shadows changing throughout the day. Abundant Rorschachs for me to interpret. The first vision I saw had me running and playing and active again. I actually saw myself as a young deer leaping effortlessly through a forest. After a while, I had only to lift up my eyes and I would see myself bouncing along, alive with graceful movements and amazing speed. Then I saw myself having friends, and laughing again, and climbing trees. After a few months of ceiling gazing, I pictured myself going to college and becoming a husband and father someday. I even envisioned myself as a doctor.

My nurse Susan convinced me that if I would keep rehearsing my vision on the ceiling, sooner or later my body would begin to move again and make it all happen. I never doubted her. At the very time when my body was at its all-time low, I trusted her to coach me toward my highest self. Knowing my eyeballs were my only moving part, she brought a projector into my room and flashed stories and pictures on the ceiling for me to consider as I pondered my future. She projected a checkerboard and taught me how to play checkers and chess as she facilitated a learning environment for my future. She would read me books while instructing me to find my life in the patterns overhead. She brought me music to listen to, and the Braille recordings of famous books. Slowly but surely I began to feel the world of sound and sight open up before me.

She obtained my school assignments for the fourth and fifth grades and tutored me without my even knowing I was doing schoolwork. Honoring my wish to become a medical doctor, Susan procured the graduate bulletins of Yale, Harvard, and Columbia medical schools. She deciphered the undergraduate prerequisites and distilled the learning process into my age group. Before leaving the hospital she had engaged me with advanced mathematics, the French language, philosophy, and English literature. I felt so privileged to be learning so much I imagined that everyone in my class was in a hospital somewhere—with polio—learning from nurses like Susan!

Before contracting polio, I had not been much of a student. My family was struggling to survive the Depression and World War II, and I was squeezed in between a brother a year older and a sister a year younger. Life was a constant scramble, day by day. My father worked in a pharmaceutical manufacturing plant, and my mother worked part-time as a clerk in a drug store.

But during my months in the hospital, in my desperate physical condition, time was all I had, second after second, and I wanted to learn everything I could. I wanted to become everything I could become. And I believed magically that what I envisioned on the ceiling would come to pass. Everything I imagined seemed possible, and what did I have to lose? Except for me, the room was silent and empty. I had no radio and TV had not yet been invented. Thank God! It took great gobs of silence to find my soul and invent my future.

One day, as I was entranced in a forest walk along the cracks in the ceiling, I felt a wiggle in the toes of my left foot. It was not much, but it was *everything*. I could move my toes, a little. When Susan made her rounds, she assured me that this was the beginning of my future unfolding—not merely my getting well but my visions being realized. She said my strength would slowly return up my legs, my backbone and arms, and finally my upper neck and chin. "You are now in training," she would say, "so practice moving your foot for the rest of the month." She tied a string to my toes up through an eyelet she screwed into the ceiling (and I winced when she made a hole in the secret garden of my mind's eye), and secured a small bell to it. "Ring the bell," she insisted, and indeed I did, having no knowledge of Pavlov and his dog.

I was astounded that Susan knew the path to my

recovery and transformation. She placed twine around my foot, up through a pulley (screwed into the ceiling!) and down to a handle on a casement window to my right. "Frederic," she whispered. "Make the window go open and closed until it makes so much noise that every nurse on the floor scolds you." High motivation for a nine-year-old, and although I was unable to move my foot for weeks or months, my attention was completely riveted to doing so. In time, it happened, and only years later did I learn that all the nurses were instructed by Susan to rush into my room to complain royally. In time, my room looked like a gymnasium, with ropes going in various directions to engage my awakening limbs with necessary exercise. I loved my room, and I had no intention of ever leaving. As ugly and bereft as it was, it was my secret garden. Never before had I been so awake, alive, and ready to soar. The last things to cooperate were my neck and upper chest, and although I still can't touch my chin to my chest, I have been eternally grateful for everything I learned and became in my recovery. I now walk, run, plan tennis, and live without any noticeable deficit.

The hardest thing I ever did was to leave that room. I cried in anguish as my wheelchair left the hospital for my uncle's farm, where I was quarantined to learn to walk again. My loneliness there was punctuated by the deadly, daily visits of an orthopedic nurse who made me exercise, without any of the mentoring Susan commanded. It was months before I could walk, but when I did, I reentered my family system and schooling as someone with a vision of where I was going and how I would get there. I had a purpose and I planned my life around it. Susan's voice continued for years as a refrain in my head: vision, plan, train, and become the best that you can be.

I did not fully grasp what Susan had taught me until midlife, when I was struggling mightily with my path and life course. By then I had shifted from becoming a doctor of medicine to becoming a doctor of philosophy. After earning a Ph.D. at Columbia University—one of the schools recommended by Susan—I became a professor of philosophy at Colby College in Maine, and then at the University of San Francisco. I also became a husband and a father. I wrote some books, became a good public speaker, and "arrived" at the goals I had conjured up with Susan.

In my late thirties, when my youth felt spent, I thought my life was over. I was out of vision. After much soul-searching, I returned to what I had learned from Susan—to be visionary and responsible for my own future. Since I remained close friends with Susan until her death in 1989, I phoned to get her advice, and this is what she blurted out: "Yesterday's dreams are not always tomorrow's promises, Frederic. Gaze at the sky above you as if you were in the hospital again, and get a new fix on where you are going, and why. What we need at midlife is not always what we wanted when we were young. But find the fire, the passion, the hope that belongs to you. It's always up there, ready to be loaned to the right person at the right time." I cried with joy.

So again I learned, painfully, to gaze at the ceiling of my life to find new paths into my future. I am telling my story so every reader can benefit from Susan's simple wisdom:

- See how you want your life to unfold.
- Look for your best choices.
- Trust your vision.
- Create a detailed plan to get you from here to there.

- Take full responsibility for your life course: time manage every detail.
- Find the best resources available for empowering your future. Network, train, travel, seek, adventure.
- Learn how to learn, unlearn, and relearn. Make learning your central business.
- Live on the outer edge of your possible reaches, not on the inner edge of your security.

Thank you, Susan!

FOREWARD

How You Will Benefit from this Book

A LifeLaunch is the beginning of a new chapter of your life. Each LifeLaunch requires fresh vision, new plans, and inner courage as you shift gears from yesterday's commitments to tomorrow's possibilities.

Because of the intense turbulence of virtually everything in the 2000's, you will probably have many more chapters in your life than your parents and grandparents had. Each of your chapters will probably be shorter than theirs, but you will have more opportunities than they to change your career, geographic locations, and adult roles. To be a happy camper in today's world, you need to know how to LifeLaunch whenever necessary or desirable.

Each LifeLaunch is a graduation from one era of your life into the next. Society used to tailor our LifeLaunches for us, and guide us down established paths of adult life. No more. Today you must design your own path, and take charge of all your LifeLaunches no matter what your age or situation.

May you live all the days of your life.
—Jonathan Swift

The first adult LifeLaunch occurs for most of us in our twenties, when we leave home or college to assume full responsibility for our lives. The only other adult LifeLaunch celebrated by the entire culture is retirement. In between, most of us make several LifeLaunches, without clear maps to guide us. This book provides you with five maps for guiding yourself successfully through all the adult territory. You will learn how to design and plan, proactively, for several new LifeLaunches between your twenties and your retirement, and after retirement as well.

With over half of our nation now beyond the "young adult years," mastery of midlife and elderhood has more urgency and importance than ever before. This book will help you plan all of your years with new skills and confidence. You will identify the best paths for your journey into challenging life/career choices. If you apply to your life the five maps contained in this book, you will evolve clear life plans for successful LifeLaunches for the rest of your life—from the springtime of young adulthood to the autumn years of elderhood.

Your past cannot be changed, but you can change tomorrow by your actions today.
—David McNally

You need a set of tools to shape, execute, and monitor each of your LifeLaunches. Those tools are in this book, along with explicit directions on how to use them.

~ Each LifeLaunch integrates the themes of work, love, family, leisure, and social commitments in new ways, as you move into your future.

~ You will understand how "change" can work to your advantage—at work, at home, and in your personal life.

~ You will tap your passion for living your best choices for the years ahead.

Suggestions

~ Use this book as you would a personal journal. Read it slowly, a little bit at a time. Meditate on the themes that speak to you. The salient concepts are deliberately restated throughout the book so you won't lose sight of the essential ideas. Interact with what you read. Write your own thoughts in a companion notebook or journal that you create as you read this book. A paper trail of your ideas is the best medium for constructing an inspired plan for your future.

~ Before you begin each chapter of the book, look at the outline provided in the Table of Contents which will help you get an overview of what is being presented. The

Index will also help you find items in the book useful for your LifeLaunch.

~ In each chapter, concentrate first on understanding the ideas being presented. Then apply them to your life through the questions and exercises provided for your personal reflection and application. Read each question as if it has your name on it. If it engages you and fits your needs, work it through in your notebook, in writing, so you can keep track of your thoughts. If any item does not speak to you, read on.

~ If you are married or living with a partner, consider reading the book together so you both can talk about how you want the next few years to be. A committed "couple" is often the best unit for planning the future during the adult years, validating your "separate" as well as your "together" plans.

~ Talk with close friends about your findings as you read along, so you get feedback, validation and encouragement as you evolve a plan. If you have a number of friends wanting to construct new life plans, set up a study group that meets every couple of weeks, taking a chapter at a time. This book is an excellent tool for group discussion and discovery—at home, work, or church.

~ Stay with the book to the very end because the ideas you discover—chapter by chapter—will guide you systematically to your emerging plans and next LifeLaunch.

Section I

Prepare to Journey Ahead

CHAPTER 1

What is the Future You Want?

Beyond Future Shock

The future doesn't drop into our laps—prefabricated—the way it used to, when society programmed "the American way" for just about everyone. In today's chaotic swirl, you get the future you want by making it happen.

We call it "entrepreneuring the future," taking responsibility for your life direction as fully as you can, within a world of constant surprises. The world you face is a dizzy flow of shifting options, so in order to shape your preferred future, you need to know what you really want, and then try to make it happen.

To have the future you prefer, you compose, design, invent, and weave the next chapter of your life, family, and career—using the abundant resources which are available by-products of global change. If you refuse to initiate your own path, your choices will be the leftovers from those around you who did entrepreneur their futures, and put you to work for their destinies.

If you want a future with your name on it, then dream a dream, construct a plan, and make "you" happen. Your ability to sort out what belongs on your path from what doesn't is perhaps the most important ability you have.

Even if you have explicit goals and objectives, you have to keep reevaluating them and adapting them as situations around you change. The good news is that you have more paths to consider than ever before. The bad news is that you have less predictability about where your decisions will lead you. Our world today has more possibilities and less surety for everyone on earth free to make choices. That's the way it will be for the twenty-first century—more choices, along with less control and reduced predictability.

As life proceeds over years, much stays the same, but more changes—a blending of many sources, a process never fully finished, a flow of beginnings and endings. You are all the time coming together and falling apart, holding on and letting go—in several dimensions and directions of your life, simultaneously and continuously.

It doesn't happen all at once...You become. It takes a long time.
—Margery Williams

The daily pressures to act, to do, to decide, make it difficult to stop and think, to consider, and to examine your life goals, directions, and priorities—to find the best choices you have for managing your own world.
—Roy Menninger

Adults are living about twenty-five years longer than adults at the beginning of the twentieth century. Those twenty-five extra years come at the end of your life, so if you're going to be potent, awake, and happy in your old age, you need to know **how**—at your present age—to develop your emerging strengths through the years ahead. Few of us know how to grow older with increased lucidity and expectancy. This book is an effort to unleash that knowledge.

If you don't know where you're going, anywhere will do, and the push-pulls of life around you will shape your path—to somewhere you haven't chosen but have to adjust to. You can do better! Choose your destinations carefully, set your sails, find your crew, use your compass, and venture forth to make your best future happen.

The secret to a resilient life in our kind of world is in knowing how to recycle yourself, over and over, letting go of what is no longer you, taking on new strengths, and shaping new chapters for your life, guided by your own emerging vision. "What we're seeking is an experience of being alive," declared Joseph Campbell, "so that we actually feel the rapture of being alive."

You are the only one who can open the doors into the next chapter of your life. After all, it's your LifeLaunch. Use this book carefully and deliberately, to link your life to your vital dreams and possibilities. Keep a pen and notebook handy as you read, and write out your own thoughts, concerns, and priorities whenever they occur to you.

The more faithfully you listen to the voice within you, the better you will hear what is sounding outside. Only he who listens can speak.
—Dag Hammarskjold

Backing into the Future

You probably burst into your post-adolescent years with great excitement, but felt unprepared for the long haul ahead. When we trade in our early years for older ones, we enter alien adult territory. We all grow older feeling terrorized by the mirror, surer of how our bodies are changing than how our lives are progressing. We *know* who we were, but we have to *imagine and believe* who we're becoming. That takes vision, trust, and courage.

Even in our thirties or forties we may feel that the gates are closing on our youthful expectations rather than opening up to the rest of our lives. We all revel in the joys of youth, but few are expectant with the joys of getting older, even if all that "older" means is that you're not as young as you were. Few of our early dreams extend very far into our mature years, and when they run out, our expectancy usually shrinks and shrivels. Most of us run out of script long before we die.

Only through intense personal effort do you learn that every closing gate is also the beginning of a new life adventure you are never fully prepared to take. You always have opportunities for blending each ending into a new beginning if you have imagination and skills for writing new script for your life—to begin a new life chapter. Shifting gears from chapter to chapter in your life is a critical life skill, particularly if you want to seize your optimal choices for the years ahead.

The secret to every LifeLaunch is looking ahead, to be visionary with the time and space in front of you as you get older and more experienced at life. All you have is time, so measure your life deliberately and learn from it constantly. Refuse to be trapped or limited by your past and your youth. Your past is a launching pad, not a fence; a school, not a prison. Your future begins with what you do today to make tomorrow happen—to dream and be courageous with your life so you can become "more." Learn how to lean into the wind.

The key is to put your energy into anticipating life rather than into fixing the problems of your past. The single, most important ingredient to a successful life is to remain proactive—to concentrate upon prospective, vital, enchanting options—and mapping your way into "tomorrow" with deliberate decisions, risk-taking, realism, and caution.

The people who get on in this world are the people who get up and look for the circumstances they want, and, if they can't find them, make them.
—George Bernard Shaw

Being an adult is an evolving thing, and most adults are amazingly uninformed about their own potential throughout the long haul of grown-up living. That is why this book on LifeLaunching is so important. This book describes the contours of adult life and how you can chart your journey ahead with both confidence and concrete plans.

Refrain of a Working Mom

When you're immersed in a family and career, it's virtually impossible to plan your own life. "How can I ever find time, day to day, for *my* future?" is a familiar refrain of working moms who look at this material.

There is no denying that a "plan" for a working mom is a far different proposition than the development of a plan for a typical working father or a working woman without children. The difference is **sheer time**.

I—Pam—am a working mom, with three children under the age of fourteen, entrepreneuring my career while moving headlong into midlife. I often become mired down when I ponder "the next chapter of my life," because my life is so wrapped up in the lives of others. Yet I want to be clear about my life and to chart my way ahead, even as I am so caught up in a never-ending three ring circus all around me.

Or perhaps even more so because of the continual drivel of chaos and maintenance. I need to be clear about a mission/goal in my life that transcends laundry, school lunches, after school activities, and bedtimes—in order to invest well in these continual demands.

My conclusion is that plans for persons like me must be tentative, yet definite; short-term, yet possible. Working moms must not stop living, dreaming, and designing their own lives. Even though much must be postponed, something should always be in the planning basket, ready to hatch. Without that we lose our zeal for life, our vitality, our love for ourselves.

We cannot live the afternoon of life according to the programme of life's morning; for what was great in the morning will be little at evening, and what in the morning was true will at evening have become a lie.
—Carl Jung

The rest of this chapter is devoted to stories of adults who have struggled with changes in their lives. The stories of Jim, Gloria, Charlie, and Martha are addressed to you, to share their experience of a LifeLaunch. The descriptions of Jim and Gloria are brief vignettes of adults who have not adapted creatively to change. Charlie and Martha are examples of persons who learned and grew as they worked through the stuck points of their lives.

Jim

If one's destiny is shaped from within, then one has become more of a creator, has gained freedom. Here one acts as subject, author, creator.
—Allen Wheelis

Jim, an executive in his fifties, is not very different from the way he was in his twenties. He works hard, makes good money, and invests carefully. He's always busy looking for more, more, more of what he's always wanted. That's his life, his script, his story.

Even though he has mastered the challenges of the first forest he entered as a young man, he hasn't journeyed further to find the clearings deeper in the woods. He still lives and dreams as if he were twenty-five—rushing about, solving problems, and organizing the world around his entry-level priorities and skills.

He hasn't internalized the advantages of his age and experience. He hasn't asked new questions or explored the emerging currents of his own life. He hasn't challenged his ego or laughed at his narcissism. He hasn't knocked on the doors of his imagination to explore who he truly could become, in midlife and beyond.

Two months ago Jim was let go by his company. Even though his benefit package was more than fair, Jim was undone. His work had been his life. His past was all he knew. How could he start all over? Within days he was depressed and at the beginning of a profound transition which would prepare him for the rest of his life.

Gloria

Gloria, who married early and devoted her life to raising three children, hasn't known what to do with herself since her children left home. She feels abandoned by her familiar world and out of sync with the career worlds of her new female friends. Rather than use her past as a resource for her future, she feels contained and limited by who she used to be. She wants to find fulfillment but her only developed talent is caretaking. Although Gloria feels trapped in her own agenda, she doesn't know how to break out into the world of money, careers, and unabashed leadership. She feels "less" because she has not explored "more."

Charlie and Martha

Charlie and Martha seemed to have it made. Everyone thought Charlie was successful. At age 44, he had a good salary, a managerial position, a new marriage with a step-family blend of four kids, and a fairly nice house in the suburbs. In his fifth year at a computer firm, he was respected and admired. He thought of himself as successful until an economic downturn struck and his firm began to panic and downsize. For sixteen months Charlie worked harder than ever before—around the clock as though a major war were under way.

Then a bell went off in his head, and he found himself daydreaming much of the time—evaluating his path and searching for answers to questions he had never asked before—about life priorities, family time, his career, and the future. Until then he had devoted his life to just "doing his best" with whatever was on his platter—particularly his career roles. He had loved challenge and brass rings, and had always wanted more. More! Now he wanted a different formula. *"No matter how things turn out at the office, I want my life from now on to be different than in my twenties and thirties. As much as I love my work, I want more time for living—more quality time with things I care deeply about. Somehow I want to become more "whole," but how? And how can I make significant changes without losing what I have already achieved?"*

Charlie spent months pondering his deeply-held values, his triumphs and trouble spots, his unused abili-

To keep alive and effective, you anticipate difficulties and opportunities. You adapt, changing and growing as the individuals and the world around you change, and you periodically recommit yourself to your mission. You act to preserve what is best and discard the rest… Developing a mission means seeing a pattern in the things and thoughts that get you moving; assessing your resources; then formulating your feelings into words.

—Charles Garfield

ties, and his latent dreams. His life review took much longer than he wanted before he evolved a definite plan that built solidly upon his past yet give him a different future.

When he was finished evaluating his life, he felt vital again and was able to negotiate most of the changes he wanted without a midlife crisis or emotional confusion. He talked it over, in depth, with his wife, Martha, his children, and friends. This was his new life plan:

~ Charlie decided to start his own small business where he could be his own person, instead of being a cog in somebody else's wheel.

~ He created a weekly schedule of home and work commitments and planned out his calendar for a whole year, including weekly events with the kids and three major trips alone with Martha. He joined an athletic club and renewed his love for tennis.

~ He described his new beginning like this: "I feel like one person again, highly motivated and much more at peace with myself. My priorities are clearer than they have been in years, and they come from deep within me. Even though I know it won't be easy to keep my new life in balance, it's my life. I am—at last—marching to my own drum, connected to what I love most, and I am one hundred percent committed to the directions I'm now taking. Frankly, that's all that matters."

Charlie had designed the scenario he wanted to make happen, created a plan and time-line, and begun a new chapter in his life. He accepted full responsibility for his choices. He was on course through conscious dreaming, planning, and courageous actions. He was entrepreneuring his future.

Martha was extraordinarily busy—with family, house, career, friends, and commuting. As a human resources professional at a firm about an hour from her house, where she had worked for twelve years, she had her hands full, not to mention her life as wife, mother, and householder.

Is there something in your life you would like to change? If so, first change your perception of the problem. When you can see yourself and your situation differently, you have already taken on the responsibility for your success.
—Marilee Zdenek

"Frankly," she confided, "managing a step-family of four kids between the ages of seven and eighteen is my most difficult job. Charlie does his best to help, but he just isn't there most of the time. I've got to be here, and so I work it out. But I feel exhausted, overextended, and out of synch much of the time. Sometimes it seems that all I do is help others live their lives. And that's got to change. But how? And when?"

As Charlie planned his future, Martha did the same, to arrive at some new formula for balancing her life. She loved all the parts but felt they didn't add up to HER. This became her new life plan:

~ Martha decided that for the next five years, she wanted to be at home more and at work less, even if it meant less money. She saw this as a temporary decision, and she wondered what the impact on her career would be. "Will I be able to realize my promise and become the leader I always believed I could be," she wondered, "or will I be more complete if I settle for less?" For now, at least, her decision was to downshift her schedule, to downsize her commitments, and to upscale her personal agenda.

~ Martha rearranged her time at work. That was the really big item. Her boss was surprisingly receptive to her recommendation that she go on a two-day work week in the office, and work one other day from her home.

~ She also decided to join a reading group to put her in touch with new friends and ideas.

~ She enrolled in a yearlong leadership training program for women, to give her an opportunity to evaluate her real leadership abilities and interests, and to provide her with an "ace" on her resume, should she need it if and when she returned full-time to the workforce.

~ Martha planned out family trips for a year in advance, hired more help to manage the household, and after a few months on that new schedule, she was in charge of her life again. The many parts of her life were more balanced, and for the first time in fifteen years she

Our lives are a series of births and deaths: we die to one period and must be born to another. We die to childhood and are born to adolescence; to our high-school selves and (if we are fortunate) to our college selves; we die to our college selves and are born into the 'real' world; to our unmarried selves and into our married. To become a parent is birth to a new self for the mother and father as well as for the baby.
—Madeleine L'Engle

had the beginning of a private life—which benefited everyone, including Charlie.

~ Martha challenged Charlie to see their new directions as something more than moving checkers to different places on the board. "I want us to be a total team in everything," she urged, "so that you know—as I do—which of our children needs to go where to be with whom each day, so you can interchange with me with any of the multitude of tasks that have to get done to make our family and home work. OK?" And while Charlie said he would do his best, they both knew that he had stretched himself about as far as he knew how—for now—and that his new business was going to be the central event in the next chapter of his life, as it had always been for him.

Overall, however, they both felt considerable progress, individually and as a couple. They had evaluated their lives and charted paths that contained both continuities and changes. They believed they had broken the bonds of slavery to everything the world wanted them to be and were writing their own stories around quality choices— creating their own new adventures on their own terms.

Like Charlie and Martha, you can chart your journeys ahead by using this book to chart your future, to make a plan and to be "on course" again. Begin your LifeLaunch with the questions that follow:

Too many young people—of all colors, and all walks of life— are growing up today unable to handle life in hard places, without hope, without adequate attention, and without steady internal compasses to navigate the morally polluted seas they must face on the journey to adulthood.
—Marion Wright Edelman

Your Turn!

1. List five things you really enjoy doing (bike riding, talking with a friend, playing tennis, cooking a gourmet meal, being close and intimate, reading a book, coaching a team, being at home, working hard, traveling, jogging, etc.). This list is a great beginning for getting ready for the future. How can you make these five activities more important in your next chapter?

2. Conduct a career review, assessing your satisfaction and dissatisfaction with your work life and prospects. Write out your evaluation in this format:
~ List what you like and want to keep doing in your job or career.

~ List what you don't like and don't want to keep doing in your job or career.

~ List how you want your career to look five years from now—personal roles, rewards, challenges.

3. Choose at least two questions from below that you find very important at this time in your life. Write out your first thoughts.

~ How can I move from getting ready to live to really living?

~ How can I deepen my connections to those I love most, and still be me?

~ How can I be at my best as a spouse and parent as my family matures?

~ How can I be more caring and sensitive to my parents' needs?

~ How can I find work that is a calling, and not merely a source of money?

~ How can I find more balance in my life?

CHAPTER 2

Your Number One Issue
Managing Uncertainty

The America I Knew, Growing-Up

When I—Frederic—grew up, I didn't feel much change in my life. Oh, change was there—the depression, World War II, and all that. But it didn't affect my life very much. At that time, the American culture was isolated from the world, and fairly uniform throughout the country.

For most people, life is a search for a proper manila envelope in which to get themselves filed.
—Clifton Fadiman

I grew up in a small city in upstate New York. When my father had severe financial problems in the 30s, my mother went to work, even as she continued to do all of the housework and cooking. Our church and close friends provided us with personal support as we struggled to make life work. The forces of stability far outweighed the forces of instability, and we treated our problems as temporary nuisances rather than as permanent threats to our lives.

World War II caused heightened anxiety throughout the community, yet had little negative effect on anyone I knew. The war, after all, took place far away, and we didn't get instant reports, as we do today. Furthermore, the quality of our lives got much better during and after the war, not worse. As the economy prospered during the war, my parents were able to purchase new clothes, an automatic washing machine, and a much better used automobile. During my growing-up days, "change" meant mostly improvement and benefits—that life was getting better.

Meanwhile, the world around me seemed uniformly one-dimensional, and I didn't think it could or would ever change. Everybody seemed remarkably alike to me, and everyone knew the seldom spoken rules guiding us all. Even school children across the country read the same books, and had the same reference points in their heads.

Family was a big part of my life. We ate all three meals together, each day. There were no school lunches in those days, so my father, who worked close by, faithfully picked up my brother, sister, and me each noon, dashed home where a simple meal was prepared for us by my mother, after which we were whisked back to school and my father returned to his work. Supper was a formal meal in our dining room, and a basic rule was never to miss it, and to remain at the table until dismissed. Some of our best family talks happened during the supper hour.

Everyone I knew went to church every Sunday, whether they liked it or not, and I was on the church baseball and basketball team. Church was a universal reference point for virtually everyone; it served as a common source of social contact, literacy, and predictable rebellion.

Although my family spent all the major holidays at my maternal grandmother's house sixty miles away, together with my cousins, aunts, and uncles, we didn't travel anywhere further until I was 17 when I made it to the Atlantic ocean for a swim—at a family reunion. That was my first occasion to stay in a "cabin," which were what existed along some highways before motels were invented.

In the world I grew up in, it was most unusual for anyone to change residence, much less move to a different part of the country. We stayed in the same house for 15 years. Almost all my childhood friends were part of my life from kindergarten through high school, when we split to the four winds. Leaving home was a major shifting of gears for me, and for most of my friends.

My parents, who had very little in the way of worldly goods, complained very little. That was another rule back then, not to complain about your lot in life. In a sense they were passive and compliant. They were also expectant and hard-working. They would say they were obedient and doing their duty, I suppose. They lived as they—and everyone around me—were programmed to live: work hard, love your family, go to church, be nice, avoid conflict, and believe in the future.

For "media" experience at home we had only newspapers and the radio until I was 17, when we got our first,

Life is not the way it's supposed to be. It's the way it is. The way you cope with it is what makes the difference.
—Virginia Satir

monster-sized TV console, with a tiny black and white screen. There weren't many programs, however, and I was unimpressed. I'd rather lie on the floor listing to radio programs like "The Shadow," "Jack Benny," or "The Lone Ranger." From age 12 on I was able to go to one movie a week, each Saturday afternoon. I would walk to the show, which was usually a Roy Rogers or Gene Autry western. The main environment of my life was not the media; it was home-school-community.

That was it! Life was remarkably uniform, predictable, safe (we didn't even lock the back door), and boring. We expected someone to tell us what to do, and they did—the president, the mayor, dad's boss, my teachers, the police, the minister, the Boy Scout leader, and—of course—my parents. When someone in authority told you what to do, you did it, more or less. We didn't curse in front of adults, nor did we hear cursing or sexual overtones from movies, radio programs, or adults around us. We were programmed to grow into bigger shoes.

There were unspoken rules about everything, and while I didn't like most of them, I stayed within the lines. Those who didn't, didn't get very far in life. It was compliance with the rules, not deviance, that was rewarded. Compliance led to reliance. The word "change" was not in vogue back then, but when it was invoked it generally meant to pull some irregularity into the greater order that surrounded our lives. Change was a temporary intrusion in our ho-hum world.

I thought, as I grew up, that America would always be as I experienced it—a moralistic straight jacket that would, nevertheless, get me to wherever I wanted to go with my life. Little changed around me in my first twenty years, so I expected that little ever would. I was conditioned to make my life work within the status quo structures, external authorities, rules, and laws—and while I yearned to rebel and cut my own path, I knew that the price of deviance was to be denied the future I could have by complying.

Change cannot be avoided.... Change provides the opportunities for innovation. It gives you the chance to demonstrate your creativity.
—Keshavan Nair

Moreover, in my heart of hearts, I believed that the world around me *was* definite and predictable, and that I should put my attention into finding my niche. In the 50s my generation received its name: the silent generation. Even as the label was pasted onto us, we didn't object!

What I didn't know as I was growing up was that I was experiencing the culmination of one era in our society, and that I would spend the rest of my life on the front edge of a very different social milieu—characterized by global issues, endless diversity, technological transformations, and constant social turbulence. The age of uncertainty had begun.

Have you ever had an eye examination? The doctor puts lens after lens in front of each eye until you say you can see clearly. An era is a bunch of lenses that all the people in a culture look through to see clearly. These lenses provide people the perception of the world that fits the cultural beliefs of the era. People who share a culture or society perceive the world much the same.

Most Americans in the first half of the 20th century looked at the world through lenses prepared to see evolving stability, progress, and the American dream. And much of the time it worked well, to produce remarkable and productive industrial growth, prospering families, and thriving communities. People everywhere thought that our culture was prepared and even destined to monitor the LifeLaunches of every red-blooded American who would work and be honest. That is how it seemed as I grew up, as I perceived the world through the eyes of the culture of that time.

During the past forty years or so that picture of American life has given way to a vastly different one. The lenses that we now see through are change, change, change. People today see the world as challenging and demanding, but also bewildering and overwhelming. The forces of change seem to have no containment, limits, or predictable sources of control. This perception of the world leads us to feel uncertain about our lives and society. And if you are uncertain for very long you begin

The reasonable man adapts himself to the world. The unreasonable man persists in trying to adapt the world to himself. Therefore all progress depends on the unreasonable man.

—George Bernard Shaw

to believe that the culture you are in is—in fact—declining and becoming dysfunctional. This, in turn, fosters cynicism, fear, and hopelessness.

Those of us still wearing the old lenses have increasing difficulty seeing the astounding advantages of the new paradigm—global flow, new markets, worldwide civilization, diversity of peoples, new careers, technological innovations, transnational political structures.

It is not our nation that is in decline; it is our outmoded beliefs and expectations about stability and progress that are keeping us from seeing the advantages of living in our current environment. It is not too late to help one another see the future as a promise rather than a burden, to see the ready assets of our times instead of the liabilities of our governments and institutions.

In a world of complex change, we need to have skills to LifeLaunch our own lives through the peaks and valleys of our cultural turbulence. Few have those skills.

The stream of creation and dissolution never stops.... All things come out of the one, and the one out of all things.
—Heraclitus

The Age of Uncertainty

The age of uncertainty began around 1973 and we're still in the early phases of it, as more and more aspects of our lives experience the world as flow. The invasion of global change in our lives often makes us feel like aliens in our own backyards. Increasingly, events we seemingly have no control over exert considerable influence on our priorities and destiny. It is like urban life arriving full-blown in Dorothy's Kansas, via television, radio, and high technology. Our experience of random flow is beyond personal, community, corporate, and national control.

I—Pam— grew up in the rural Midwest on land my grandparents homesteaded—in a house surrounded at a few miles distance by families which we all knew for at least three generations of history. I remember one of my greatest fears when I left to attend a university of ten thousand students was that I would not know the families and histories of the people I would choose as friends.

Today I live in an urban neighborhood where I don't know much of anything about the people living on either side of our home. I barely keep up with the pace of change all around me and my husband and my children. I struggle to program my answering device on the phone, and I've given up on VCR taping.

We are now daily buffeted about by a random, disruptive flow of the unexpected. We are endlessly reacting to issues and factors we did not realize would affect us directly—technological innovations, a world-wide recession, troubles in the Middle East and Africa, civil war in the former Yugoslavia, chaos in Russia, and drifting homeless in the United States. Most of us are untrained to make sense of our lives or our culture today.

It is all too easy to get the impression that the world as we've known it is falling apart. We learn it from TV, and from the radio, only to be repeated in the movies. It fills newspapers and magazines. Bad news sells, and we become mesmerized by endless global crises that we can't do much about. We pipe crisis after crisis into our living rooms and bedrooms, and then into our brains and lives. The world may be no worse than it ever was, but thanks (or no thanks) to technology and the media, more of us than ever before in history consume as our central diet shocking stories about violence, misery, and human failings from all over the globe.

Yet that same technology brings us amazing new learning tools and programs that nourish the human soul. Let's face it: you have a choice. You don't have to watch thousands of people get killed on television, or endless interpretations of the latest world tragedy. You can "be informed" and still spend more time reading, obtaining new skills through training programs, visiting local mu-seums and art galleries, or serving some cause you believe in. It all depends on how you see the world and your future within it.

One way leads you to feel less empowered and more passive and helpless. The other way—taking change as the fundamental prism—leads you to feel that the human feast has expanded and is more accessible to more people, but this requires strong personal monitoring of the limit-less number of opportunities and dilemmas presented to us.

We can never be really prepared for that which is wholly new. We have to adjust ourselves, and every radical adjustment is a crisis in self-esteem; we undergo a test, we have to prove ourselves. It needs inordinate self-confidence to face drastic change without inner trembling.
—Eric Hoffer

Changing paradigms—mental models for understanding the world around you—is always difficult for people in cultures that have prospered and become superpowers, like ancient Greece and Rome—and the United States. When you and your culture have succeeded big time, you tend to want to "hold on" to the status quo, not learn from constant change. Still, we have a choice, both as a people and at the very personal level of life planning, and your personal choice in how you see the world has immense implications for your home life, success at work, and effectiveness as a person. **The challenge is to find ways to shape your life around the flow of change, the experience of uncertainty, and the advantages of dissolving environments.**

We all know, at some level, that the American future is not going to look very much like America today. But this does not mean our lives and culture are going to be worse off overall. Our future is neither a guaranteed decline nor an incline. It's just going to be different. In all likelihood, some aspects of our lives will get beter, and some will get worse. However, we will decide, individually and collectively, if the overall impact of change on our lives increases our cynicism and shrinks our expectancy, or deepens our will-to-live and challenges our sense of purpose.

Do you feel—overall—that you are diminished or extended by the changing environments of your life? How can you get the flow of change in your life and find new promises, horizons, resources, and passions, throughout all your years? Read on to find out.

The way we see events approaching us affects the way we respond to them; the way we respond to them affects the way we regard ourselves; and this in turn affects the way we see new events.
—W. Timothy Gallwey

Your Turn!

1. What would you say has changed your life for the *better*, *improving* your life style and human prospect during the past ten years? Make a list.

2. What would you say has changed your life for the *worse*, *diminishing* your life style and human prospect during the past ten years? Make another list.

3. Whom do you know who seems to thrive on the changes taking place in our lives today? What is he or she like, and what are the specific qualities that make him or her effective in a change environment? Are these qualities you want to pursue in yourself?

4. How do you think your life will be better and worse *five* years from now?

5. In what ways are you better off and worse off than your parents? Your grandparents?

6. Imagine it is the year 2,020. What do you think will be much the same, and what will be very different? For example, how do you imagine these will be: housing, schools, your career field, marriage, child rearing, cars, public transit, TV, computers, religious institutions, the environment, wars and violence, taxes?

7. What are your ways of managing uncertainty? Think carefully about how you sustain your integrity and dreams when the world swirls around you. Write down your ideas.

CHAPTER 3

How to Keep Winning When the Rules Keep Changing

26 . . . .

Two Worlds -
My Father's and Mine

The last indelible talk I—Frederic—had with my father was in 1974, when he was a ripe sixty-seven and I had just turned forty. I was on my annual Christmas visit "home," at the end of a difficult year containing divorce, a career change, and what we would now call "a life transition." Dad seemed eager to speak his mind, and while I felt vulnerable, I was more excited than scared— wanting to connect deeply with him, again.

Human beings, by changing the inner attitudes of their minds, can change the outer aspects of their lives.
—William James

"I just don't understand," he began, as I drove his vintage Chevy up the Florida coast. "You're the first member of the family ever to divorce. And you have spent years preparing for the career you now plan to leave. My approach is that you make the most of what's already on your platter. Its just not right to give up. You worked hard to get to the top, and now you are starting all over. You'll never amount to anything that way."

"But dad," I protested, "I had no idea what I was getting into when I was younger, and now...." "Nonsense," he snapped, "you just lack commitment. That's all." I pulled the car over to the side of the road and looked him straight in the eyes as I asserted—as gently but clearly as I knew how: "My world is not like yours. You figured you had one shot at everything—one career, one marriage, one family, one home, one city, one church, one everything. Just get launched and the world takes care of you. And your world was somehow always there to steady your course. I have more choices on my platter than I know how to deal with every day—and they keep changing—from how to work to where to live. I'm not as sure as you always seemed to be about which decisions lead to what consequences." I explained that my world was more turbulent and less predictable than his, and my life more complicated than his. That I was always on duty, and always a little unsure.

"In your day," I insisted, "everybody knew the rules and most people followed them, in order to succeed and be happy. But in my world, the rules keep changing, day by day. To make my life sing, I have to live on the edge, take risks and charge ahead. I am no less committed than you, but I live by the seat of my pants, and when I hit a detour or dead-end, I've got to know how to start over. Understand?"

"No," he said slowly and sadly, his voice lowered, "your life is no different from mine. As I see it, either you fit yourself into the opportunities presented to you, stick to them, and make the most of them for the long haul, or you're going to get yourself into a heap of trouble."

Even though he thought my path was wrong, I felt I was making the right decisions in the world as I found it, which seemed remarkably different from the crystal clear world that dad thought he lived in. And what I realized, for the first time in my long struggle to justify my life to my dad, was that my life was no better and no worse than his, just as his was no better and no worse than mine. My life and my world are simply different from his life and his world. Years later he said as much to me.

We Live between Eras

It is becoming more and more difficult to connect the chapters of our lives to one another—from childhood, through the adult years, to elderhood. Our adult lives used to be programmed by more or less stable, linear conduits—careers, families, neighborhoods, churches, community organizations—that connected us as individuals to our entire life cycle. Today our lives have increasing amounts of surprises, complexity, and cynicism.

For most of the twentieth century, the world we lived in seemed fairly dependable, uniform, and evolving—and so our lives took on those dimensions. We were fairly optimistic. Today we are vividly aware—through interminable media coverage of every crisis on earth—that our world is turbulent, unpredictable, and fragile, and our lives are now internalizing those qualities. Compared with life in mid-twentieth century America, our lives today are more tentative and worried, and we are less

*And the seasons they go round and round
And the painted ponies go up and down
We're captive on a carousel of time.
We can't return, we can only look
Behind from where we came
And go round and round and round
In the circle game.*
—Joni Mitchell

optimistic and expectant. How could it be otherwise? The central force that shapes our consciousness today is change—coming at us from every direction, like global tidal waves washing away the rocks of the past.

As my wife and coauthor has said earlier, she grew up in a rural, Midwestern, farming region where the family phone number was two longs and a short, and there were eight other families using the same line. Today we live on the edge of Los Angeles exchanging information from our home via electronic mail, the internet, a fax machine, and voice mail.

In less than half a century, our perception of the world has shifted from a stable, orderly, steady-state model to an unstable, disorderly, change-driven one. Yet most of us live *as if* the steady-state model were fully operative, or ought to be. And we rage or whine when we find it isn't so. Most of us expect to have life plans that will lead us with assurance toward definite security, happiness, and financial prosperity. In the twenty-first century, that's a prescription for misery. Instead of learning how to fulfill our lives within the change process that dominates our lives and our era, we tend to view our lives as declining from the promises the generations before us lodged deeply in our minds. It's time to change the paradigm, the picture in our minds of how life works in our times.

There are four old rules that need to be replaced—in our thinking process—with four new rules. Here is a summary of the old rules and new rules:

Everything that happens to you is your teacher. The secret is to learn to sit at the feet of your own life and be taught by it.
—Polly B. Berends

The Old Rules vs The New Rules

1. The Linear Rule	1. The Circular Rule
2. The Outside-In Rule	2. The Inside-Out Rule
3. The Learning-Is-Just-for-Kids Rule	3. The Learning-Isn't-Just-for-Kids Rule
4. The Steady-State Rule	4. The Endless Change Rule

THE OLD PARADIGM
The Four Old Rules

1. The Linear Rule—This rule promised progress for those who are honest and work hard. According to this rule, our lives, careers, economy, and culture were supposed to get better and better, year by year, generation by generation—if we did our best and followed the cultural rules.

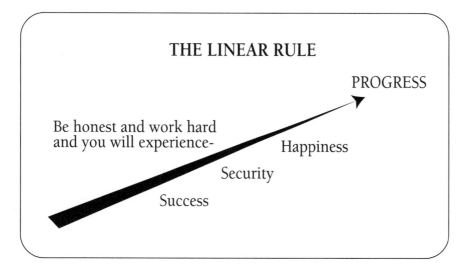

2. The Outside-In Rule—This rule said your personal life is defined and determined by the directives of the society around you. From this point of view, the boxes of life around us shaped and determined our personal choices—communities, families, work systems and the nation. Nobody talked about "life planning" because people thought their lives were already planned by the world around them.

According to this rule, to succeed as a human being, follow the advice of the systems around you: the official authorities in schools, religious organizations, work organizations, and governments. The containers of your life will keep you happy, successful, and secure, according to the outside-in rule. They are more stable, permanent, and reliant than you are, according to this rule. To be a winner, "Just do what you're told."

I have no way of knowing what results my actions will have…. My only sure reward is in my actions and not from them. The quality of my reward is in the depth of my response.
—Hugh Prather

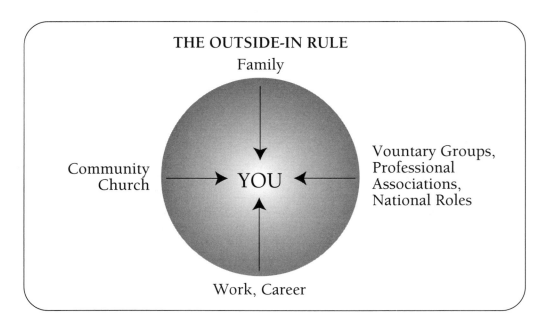

THE OUTSIDE-IN RULE
Family

Community
Church

YOU

Vountary Groups,
Professional
Associations,
National Roles

Work, Career

People are losing their faith in the future. Our education, unfortunately, molded us for a life that was always tensed toward a series of achievements—school, military service, a career, and, as a grand finale, the encounter with the heavenly father. But now our tomorrows no longer appear in that optimistic perspective. People no longer believe in a 'better tomorrow.'
—Federico Fellini

3. The Learning-Is-for-Kids Rule—In the linear world of the first half of the twentieth century, learning was the central business of children and young people, to *launch* **them into stable adult careers, family life, and leadership roles.** Once launched into the adult years, adults shifted from "learning" to "work" as their main activity. Throughout the rest of their years, training outside of work roles played a very minor role.

There was no basis for thinking that there were new skills and human competencies needing to be learned and developed throughout the lifecycle. Learning was a central function of young people, not adults—to prepare the way for the initial plunge toward success. Each of us would get molded during our younger years and then hopefully function like personal dynamos the rest of our lives. The notions that adults would need and want to learn continuously and LifeLaunch every decade or so was thoroughly foreign.

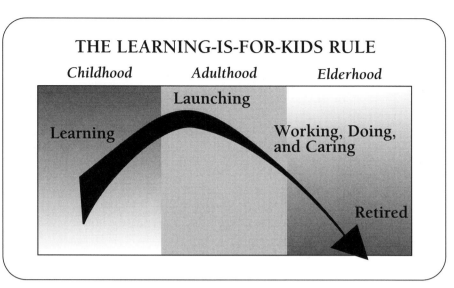

THE LEARNING-IS-FOR-KIDS RULE

Childhood *Adulthood* *Elderhood*

Launching

Learning

Working, Doing, and Caring

Retired

4. The Steady-State Rule—**This rule promised that if we worked hard we would each arrive at** *a steady-state* **or plateau of security for the rest of our lives.** That was the deal, like a cultural reward for falling into line.

When I was a boy, I thought that when I got to be about 25-30, something in me would click and I would feel like and act like all the adults I had observed as I was growing up. I saw the adult years as a steady-state period of stability, achievement, and devotion. Everyone I knew thought that there was an automatic and permanent shift when the childhood stages of development ended and the adult years began.

When I didn't get the click I thought I deserved, I behaved as if I had, and I lived as consistently as I knew how, but was greatly relieved when I discovered in my 40s that adult life for most of my friends was more like a roller coaster than like a train racing to its destination. Often, when people don't arrive at these imagined plateaus in midlife, they feel that they have failed. They often remain despondent or angry, and the problem is not in their behavior but in the belief that no longer makes sense.

Let not young souls be
smothered out before
They do quaint deeds
and fully flaunt
their pride.
It is the world's
one crime its babes
 grow dull,
Its poor are ox-like,
limp and leaden-eyed.
Not that they starve,
but starve so
dreamlessly,
Not that they sow, but
that they seldom reap,
Not that they serve,
but have no
 gods to serve,
Not that they die, but
that they die like sheep.
—Vachel Lindsay

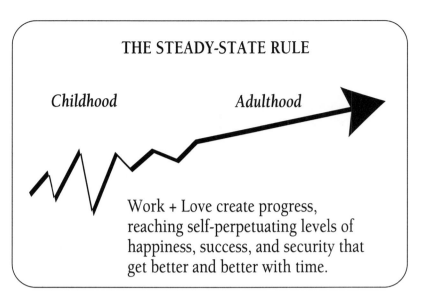

THE STEADY-STATE RULE

Childhood *Adulthood*

Work + Love create progress, reaching self-perpetuating levels of happiness, success, and security that get better and better with time.

The Cultural Shift from the Old Rules to the New Rules

Human beings have always employed an enormous variety of clever devices for running away from themselves.... We can keep ourselves so busy, fill our lives with so many diversions, stuff our heads with so much knowledge, involve ourselves with so many people, and cover so much ground that we never have time to probe the fearful and wonder-ful world within.... By middle life, most of us are accomplished fugitives from ourselves.
—John Gardner

Ever so gradually but definitely throughout the past forty years, these old rules—which thrived and worked well since the founding days of the United States—led us to a sense of decline and discouragement. The old rules require a culture high in continuity, control, and agreed-upon authority, and as those features eroded during the past few decades, we began to feel that something was wrong with us, our communities, and our governments. The more we strived to live by the old rules, the more frustrated and helpless we felt.

In and of themselves, these rules are not wrong; they simply no longer work well in the world we now live in. When people or a society hold on to beliefs and rules that are dysfunctional in their daily experience, they become angry, scared, cynical, and disempowered. Their optimism, hope, and expectations shrink until they are replaced by a pervasive pessimism. The world around them—including their own governments and corporate powers—seems less friendly and promising.

This is basically what Americans have experienced during the past several decades. Although we are without question the only superpower in the world, with many industrial, technical, and cultural superlatives, we are more tentative than ever about our manifest destiny, and less sure than ever before of the destinies of our personal lives and families.

Our cultural crisis is our loss of purpose—our confidence, hope, belief in the future. Many if not most of us live lives that are more frightened than expectant; more worried than motivated; more self-absorbed than enchanted, more indulgent than planning ahead. After the lofty adventures of the twentieth century, our balloon has lost its air and we lack the mental maps for flying confidently into the new territory of the millennium.

The way ahead is to change our expectations, our perceptions, our vision of how life works—and to come up with rules that empower our lives and institutions in the context of the rapid change that defines our time. Most of all we need to believe in ourselves again—both as individuals and as a people or culture.

If we replace the four old rules with new rules that are both fair and empowering for our lives in our kind of world, we can restore confidence, quality living, productivity, and leadership with amazing speed and effectiveness.

Much if not most of the human malaise in our country today arises from cultural maps that no longer direct us courageously into our future possibilities. Our cultural crisis is not economic decline, as we are so often told. Our central dilemma is the inadequacy of the "mental maps" we are following—the prevailing beliefs of cultural evolution and progress, the expectation of "more" and "better," the illusion of permanent "control," the belief that hard work and honesty automatically lead to happiness and success. Increasingly, Americans are realizing that for nearly half a century we've been applying outdated notions of

Go, seeker, if you will, throughout the land.... Observe the whole of it, survey it as you might survey a field. It's your oyster—yours to open if you will. Just make yourself at home, refresh yourself, get the feel of things, adjust your sights, and get the scale. Everyone has a chance, regardless of birth, achievement, golden opportunity—to live, to work, to be a self, and to become whatever his or her humanity and vision can combine to make. This, seeker, is the promise of America.
—Thomas Wolfe

human effectiveness to a world that works by a new set of rules. This book will acquaint you with new ways to find fulfillment in the territory ahead, including five maps for guiding you toward the destinations you want.

Overall, our society today is healthier than it is sick, and the quality of our lives is among the highest in the world, but we the people are no longer clear about how to find or sustain personal and social fulfillment within the world as we find it. There are new rules to learn for empowering our lives, latent in the very words we fear are our undoing: global chaos, discontinuity, and transitions. Our biggest challenge is to construct our lives and social institutions around the advantages and opportunities of the change process itself, starting with the micro systems of our lives: our lifestyles, work styles, family life, and community relationships. The four new rules that follow form a new paradigm for understanding our world today as a creative and challenging environment for our lives.

THE NEW PARADIGM
The Four New Rules

Perhaps this is the most important thing for me to take back from beach-living: simply the memory that each cycle of the tide is valid, each cycle of the wave is valid, each cycle of a relationship is valid.
—Ann Morrow Lindbergh

1. The Circular Rule—Life itself, with its recurring seasons, is a self-renewing process. Our lives today are measured by cycles and chapters, not by linear accomplishments. This rule is the best, basic model for empowering your life today.

Think of your life as a story, with many chapters. Each chapter itself has a beginning and an end, and a transition to the next chapter. Chapters are when our lives "do" something important; transitions are when our lives get renewed. That is the basic model for understanding your life in today's world. Measure your life in small units of "script" that dramatically describe who you are, with whom, and doing what. When that script becomes too rusty or wobbly to perpetuate, you ride the waves of change—called a transition, and either modify your story or come up with a new one. That's the circular rule, as you continuously ravel and unravel your life. Your life is in continuous change, and for the most part it doesn't get better or worse, it just gets different, as it forms chapter after chapter. If you view your life this way, you can feel comfortable in our kind of world, and challenged by change instead of undone by it.

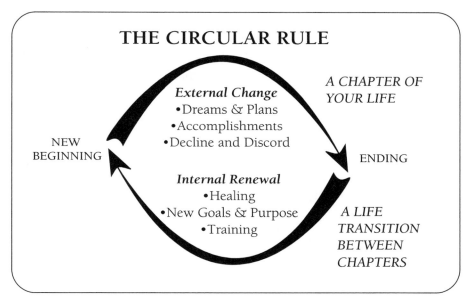

THE CIRCULAR RULE

External Change
•Dreams & Plans
•Accomplishments
•Decline and Discord

Internal Renewal
•Healing
•New Goals & Purpose
•Training

A CHAPTER OF YOUR LIFE

NEW BEGINNING

ENDING

A LIFE TRANSITION BETWEEN CHAPTERS

Applying the circular rule to your life requires high levels of personal confidence, self-responsible behavior, and trust in forces beyond your control. To use this rule, you need to know how to:

~ *Design the chapters of your life throughout all your years;*

~ *Become the leader and manager of the chapters of your life;*

~ *Embrace necessary transitions between each chapter of your life and invent the main themes and dimensions of your next chapter;*

~ *Make renewal of yourself and your social context the central features of your life.*

The circular rule is about beginnings and endings. It is about an ongoing process of self-renewal, growth, and discovery. Typically the cycle begins with a strong

For many Americans the 'revolution of rising expectations' may be simply a desire for a larger house and a second car, but for some it is a growing demand for the fulfillment of needs which are not basically material but are primarily psychological needs for a larger and more satisfying life experience.
—Angus Campbell

inclination to make something important happen and ends when that effort no longer works or seems important. Beginnings are romantic times, fostering passionate commitments. Endings require us to let go of some dream or effort that has gone stale or awry, and either to fix it or find a different one.

~ Learn how to cooperate with change, to use change as an opportunity for growth and discovery in every chapter of your life.

~ Learn how to begin each chapter of your life with feisty determination to make it succeed.

~ When your chapter is limp and exhausted, and the end is just a matter of time, design your own exit, and begin again—without whining or blaming.

~ Learn how to reconstruct your life through conscious transitions, when you seek new clarity on your priorities and choices.

2. The Inside-Out Rule—To stay "on course" in a world that is going in a thousand directions at once, you need to be value-driven and purposive. You need to be anchored in your beliefs.

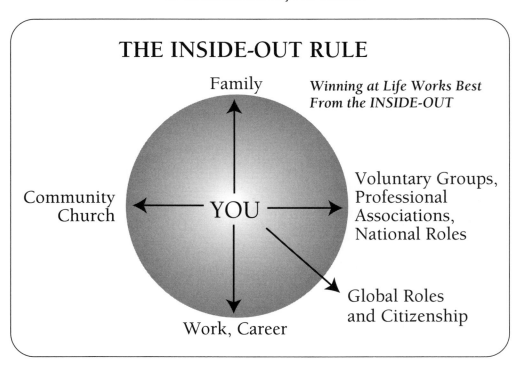

THE INSIDE-OUT RULE

Family

Winning at Life Works Best From the INSIDE-OUT

Community Church

YOU

Voluntary Groups, Professional Associations, National Roles

Global Roles and Citizenship

Work, Career

Otherwise, the winds of change will blow you in a different direction with every breeze. To succeed as a human being in the twenty-first century, you need to be living with purpose, shaping your commitments in the world around your abiding beliefs and concerns. Your many roles as an adult—at work, home, play, community and the rest—are meant to be extensions of your inner self—your core values. Stay anchored to your abiding beliefs and pursue goals you believe in.

Manage your life from the "inside-out," from your inner values and beliefs to your broader commitments and roles. Find outer resources to support your fiery purpose. Stay responsible for your destiny, and link up boldly to others in ventures you truly believe in. Become one person with many roles.

Develop a plan for staying on course that might include:

~ Choose a quiet and private place to just sit and ponder each day, or even once a week. Let your mind wander freely as you gain control of the central focus of your inner self.

~ Seek out regular contact with one long term friend who is like a mentor for you, a guide into a reliable future.

~ Try your hand at journaling, writing down your free-flowing thoughts and ideas. Doing this even once a week will open a door to your inner strength that otherwise might remain closed.

~ Get out of town alone twice this year, and go to a quiet, secluded place for renewal and discovery.

In a world that is constantly changing, there is no one subject or set of subjects that will serve you for the foreseeable future, let alone for the rest of your life. The most important skill to acquire now is learning how to learn.
—John Naisbitt

3. The Learning-Isn't-Just-for-Kids Rule—
The key to everyone's future. It's the way you stay awake throughout your adult years, getting new tools, support, and excitement. Persons who make an unwavering commitment to learning stay fresh and alert. They have new information and powerful concerns. They lead vanguard lives, knocking on the doors of tomorrow. More than any other one activity, learning

is what separates adults into two categories: the proactive and the reactive.

When you "learn," you increase your awareness, concern, and knowledge about something. You disturb your own mental stability to create positive change for

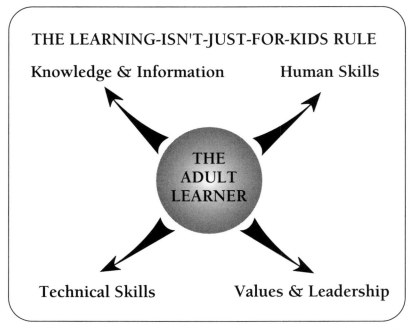

THE LEARNING-ISN'T-JUST-FOR-KIDS RULE

Knowledge & Information   **Human Skills**

THE ADULT LEARNER

Technical Skills   **Values & Leadership**

I have no doubt whatever that most people live in a very restricted circle of their potential being. They make use of a very small portion of their possible consciousness. We all have reservoirs of life to draw upon, of which we do not dream.
—William James

growth and discovery. Learning is the essence of self-renewal, the most positive form of human change. The adult learning agenda has at least four different areas under continuous exploration:

~ **Knowledge and Information:** The knowledge you acquire during your younger years is outmoded and must be replaced several times throughout your lifetime. To be awake and effective throughout your years, you have to unlearn what is no longer relevant or accurate and then learn from the creative edge of today's information explosion.

You can always create—for yourself—a learning program to become significantly better at something by the end of each month, and each year. If you do, you will actually become significantly better at many things, because the act of learning something opens you up to see, hear, and become.

~ **Human Skills**: You need more than information and knowledge to make the adult years a positive journey. You need to be an effective human generalist, to be competent at speaking, writing, listening, persuading, caring, or managing conflict. What human skills do you need to acquire or enhance to be effective in the settings where you work and live?

~ **Technical Skills**: Most of today's adults require substantial expertise within some specialty career area. We live in a technological age which is changing at a rapid pace. We don't lack opportunities to learn these evolving skills; we lack the determination to stay at the cutting edge of our fields, and to discipline our time management accordingly.

~ **Values and Leadership**: Adults perform the leadership roles in our society, and they are the bearers of culture from one era to another—through executive roles to voluntary causes to mentoring relationships. As you get older, it is natural for your learning to become more and more about values, caring, and becoming generative. Do you feel this happening in your life at this time?

What are the learning projects that might prepare you for your leadership roles? Write them down and put some of them into your plan for the next chapter of your life.

In the depth of winter, I finally learned that within myself there lay an invincible summer.
—Albert Camus

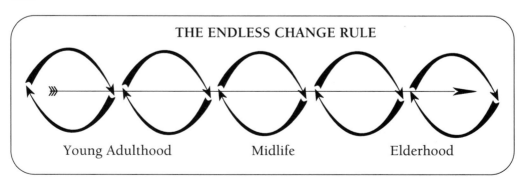

THE ENDLESS CHANGE RULE

Young Adulthood   Midlife   Elderhood

4. The Endless Change Rule—Conducting the journey is more important than the destinations, since all arrivals are temporary. There are no steady-

state resting places, only continuous change throughout all the years of our lives. People who perceive their lives as a cycle know that there is no arrival at a steady-state of crystallized happiness. Process, not progress, becomes the familiar reality.

As you get older you keep revising and renewing the same issues, the same urges, and the same concerns that you have always had—only in ever changing settings and circumstances.

You chart your way, guide your life, anticipate tomorrow, have your victories and defeats, evaluate as you proceed, change course as necessary, experience losses and gains, and assume responsibility for your destiny.

In our kind of world, competent persons need to know how to renew themselves, over and over—to knit life together whenever possible, and to unravel it when necessary. If you do that you will perceive change as a challenge—an opportunity to learn, discover, and grow.

If you can commit to what is of lasting worth while learning new directions to explore, you can thrive on change and find a future containing challenge and fulfillment.

The new rules provide dependable guidelines for finding comfort and empowerment in our kind of world. Take your time to internalize them, in your words, in your settings, for your life. Then move on to apply the five maps that follow to your own life, to see where you want to go in your LifeLaunch, and what you want to do and be in the next chapter of your life.

Life is a mystery—
unfold it.
Life is struggle—
face it.
Life is beauty—
praise it.
Life is a puzzle—
solve it.
Life is opportunity—
take it.
Life is sorrowful—
experience it.
Life is a song—
sing it.
Life is a goal—
achieve it.
Life is a mission—
fulfill it.
—Anonymous

Your Turn!

1. Imagine that you are composing your autobiography, and that you begin by constructing the basic outline of your life story. Indicate the general chapters, themes, events and characters in each chapter. Begin with some important earlier point in your life and conclude with some recent event.

Title of Book:_____

Chapter I—Title:
Dates: From about_____ to _____
        Themes
        Events
        Characters
        Ending and transition to Chapter II

Chapter II—Title:
Dates: From about_____ to _____
        Themes
        Events
        Characters
        Ending and transition to Chapter III

Chapter III—Title:
Dates: From about_____ to _____
        Themes
        Events
        Characters
        Ending and transition to Chapter IV

Chapter IV—Title:
Dates: From about_____ to _____
        Themes
        Events
        Characters
        Ending and transition to Chapter V

Chapter V—Title:
Dates: From about_____ to _____
        Themes
        Events
        Characters
        Ending and transition to Chapter VI
(Add as many chapters as you need.)

2. Now serve as your own literary critic. Ask yourself these questions:

~ What are the central themes of my life so far (for example: love, career, heroic actions, sports, adventure)?

~ What have been my "happiest," most "successful" moments?

~ What have been my most "unhappy" times or times of personal failure?

~ What were the conditions surrounding my endings and transitions (for example: relationships, getting older, career positions, loss of dreams, bad luck)?

~ What themes and events and persons are essential to the next chapter of my life?

3. How can you sustain an effective learning agenda in your next LifeLaunch, improving your human skills, technical skills, and values and leadership abilities?

~ **Human Skills**: Choose from the following any ideas that might work for you:
   —Sign on to an on-line service and communicate with others who are interested in personal skill development.
   —If you have children at home, create a study group with two or three other couples or single parents to discuss parenting issues and strategies for using the home as a learning center for everyone to learn basic human skills.
   —At work you can arrange luncheons around audio tapes and articles on human skill areas that everyone present has reviewed.
   —Spend a couple of hours each week in a good library or book store where you can browse what's being written in magazines and books.

~ **Technical Skills**: Choose from the following any ideas that might work for you:

—Use selected seminars and intensive learning
  formats, about every three months.
—Engage in disciplined study and discussion with
  colleagues.
—Pursue an advanced degree or certification programs
  to acquire further mastery in your professional field,
  or to begin defining a profession for yourself.
—Use computer resources, CD Rom, interactive technologies, and information networks to turn your
  home computer into a veritable university.

~ **Values and Leadership**: Choose from the following any
  ideas that might work for you:
—Create a neighborhood watch group of concerned
  people who are willing to keep an eye on each other's
  properties to ward off break-ins and uninvited trouble.
—Get involved in your church or club in some area
  of community concern, such as volunteer work, political activity, or getting kids or elders involved in sports.
—Take adult education courses in some area in which you
  want to make a contribution.
—Adopt a family in a third world country and learn all you
  can about their setting and situation.
—Take a leadership role in an area you are committed to.
  No matter how small or large the role—it can make a
  difference.

Section II

Consult your Compass,
Follow These Maps

CHAPTER 4

MAP 1
Composing Your Life
Chapters and Transitions

You are well on your way toward a new LifeLaunch.

You see how the rules for successful living have changed. You know that change is now the primary reality that shapes and unshapes our lives, invading our personal lives at more levels and dimensions than ever before. It is both a threat and a resource for our life designs.

You are ready to use the five maps of adult life to design the next chapter of your life.

Life is a daring adventure or it is nothing.
—Helen Keller

Map 1 will help you stay in charge of your life, whether you are up or down. You will discover how to tap the cycle of change for designing the rest of your life, to use change as a major resource for your future life designs.

Map 2 will guide you to select your current core values for shaping your next chapter, so you feel alive and purposive. You will find your compass for the journey you are about to take.

Map 3 will help you prioritize your most important "activities" and "roles" so you connect yourself to your preferred future.

Map 4 will take you on an exciting tour of the predictable changes that take place in adult lives from ages twenty to ninety, suggesting ways to take advantage of whatever your age may be.

Map 5 will evoke from you a definite learning agenda, identifying specific skills and abilities you want to master for the journey ahead.

In this chapter—Map 1—you will discover creative ways to plan your life in stable and unstable times. This map is the most important one to put to work for yourself, so you can make change your friend and enjoy your journey through flow. No matter how change is impacting you, there are ways to invest in growth, discovery, and meaning. With this map you become a change master!

You are Your Story

At the end of the last chapter you constructed an outline of your life story—chapter by chapter, event by event. In that exercise, you were the author, the main actor, and the literary critic. You are your story as you program the future, also. You extend certain themes-events-characters, and introduce new ones, as your life rolls on. You write the script and evaluate the story. The more you understand yourself as the story teller of your own story, the more you will produce new stories and script for both the next chapter of your life and the transitions between those chapters.

In the twenty-first century, all of our life stories must find comfort and congruence with increasing amounts of bewilderment and discontinuity. You need to know how to find meaning and opportunity in valleys as well as peaks, in transitions as well as the chapters of life.

All of our lives proceed in an ongoing cycle—through chapters of relative stability (which we'll call life structures) and shorter periods of relative instability (which we'll call transitions). From birth on, we measure our lives through peaks and valleys, highs and lows, stability and instability—over and over again.

Your life is an autobiography unfolding, a never-finished sculpture, a life in progress—with chapters of external achievement and accomplishment followed by periods of internal rearrangement and renewal. The temporary destinations you reach are much less important than your ability to manage and enjoy the journey itself.

If you want to be happy, put your effort into controlling the sail, not the wind.

—Anonymous

During most of the twentieth century the relative stability of our society hid this ongoing cycle of our lives. Most of us believed that our lives were measured by only one phase in the cycle of change: our external "doing"— accomplishments, success, and accumulation of money and goods. Now that society is in great turbulence, each person, family, and social unit must learn to navigate through the whitewaters of our time.

We are realizing that everyday adult life includes down time as well as up time, and that this is not a decline in our cultural history or a failure in personal performance, but rather a new way of understanding our life paths within in the realities that now frame our lives.

*All my life's a circle,
sunrise and sundown.
Moon rolls through the
nighttime till daybreak
comes around. Seasons
spring 'round again,
years keep rolling by.*
—Harry Chapin

The Pattern of All Change

There is a definite pattern to our experience of change. If you know that pattern, and where you are in it, you can identify the best choices for guiding your life, no matter how much change you are enduring.

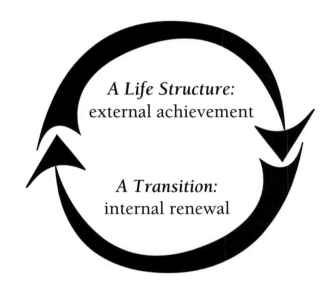

A Life Structure:
external achievement

A Transition:
internal renewal

If you are familiar with this cycle, and are comfortable with its flow, change will seem less like a destroyer and more like a conveyer of your life. If you try to contain life to the good times when the sun shines, you will feel diminished and lost when the thunderstorms begin. You become a change master when you can find meaning and purpose in all the seasons and conditions of your life. The change cycle is a renewal experience for each of us, and the systems of our lives as well.

When you were born, you were most surely in an unfamiliar environment in which you were intensely bewildered. In time you learned about a familiar world of food and being held, of sounds and sights—much of which probably revolved around your mother and father. By the end of three or four months you had experienced two sets of tools for managing change:

~ Stable behaviors—For getting through predictable, structured events, where you are oriented and committed, with familiar routines.

~ Transition behaviors—For getting through unfamiliar, unstructured events; where you are confused and disoriented, with unclear roles.

Infants and children go through several stages of development, each of which involves a transition (in which they lack confidence, behave awkwardly, and eventually discover new ways to forge a life direction) and a new period of relative stability (in which they have confidence, pursue goals, and sustain relationships). Children and adolescents experience several cycles of transitions and stable times before they leave home to enter the adult years.

Until recently, we assumed that all this came to a screeching halt when we became adults, when we supposedly arrived at steady personalities and behavioral constancy. If we had very many changes in our lives— career shifts, new geographic locations, change of mates, new interests—we were considered unstable. Something was wrong with us.

Now we realize that the rhythm of our childhood years is the basic pattern of our entire life. The ups and downs of stable times, followed by fluid transitions, shape the contours of our adult lives.

During much of the twentieth century, this normal feature of adult life was camouflaged by the entrenched stability of the family, work institutions, churches, communities, and the nation itself. Although the social fabric around us is still fairly stable and predictable, it is also looser, more fluid, and less able to assure us of lasting stability than it was a few years ago. With every part of society reeling from constant change, there is little to

Life is full of change. The good passes, but so does the bad. Nothing remains the same in this unstable world. When we are down at the bottom of the pit of despair, the only way to go is up. If we only wait a little, the cycle—the endless, unfalling tide of things, will sweep us up again. Without darkness we would not appreciate the light when it comes.
—Kristin Zambucka

buffer, hide, or absorb the natural cycle of our lives. To sustain your life, you need to be able to live creatively with stable and unstable times. The key is knowing how to cooperate with the change process itself.

Beginnings-Structures-Peaks

Committed
Outer Work
Achieving
- - - - - - - - - - - - - - - - -
Disoriented
Inner Work
Revitalizing

Endings-Transitions-Valleys

Understanding Life Chapters and Transitions

Periods of stability and structure are the "chapters" of your life, times when—for the most part—life seems mostly harmonious, purposeful, predictable, and goal-oriented.

~ This is your *outer journey* into the world around you, where you face external challenge, threats, and opportunities.

~ Stable times provide you with *opportunities for continuous roles* (wife, parent, worker, volunteer) within which you can live out a plan and produce results. You want to "do something" and arrive at success, recognition, and happiness.

It is only when we realize that life is taking us nowhere that it begins to have meaning.
—P. D. Ouspensky

A LIFE STRUCTURE

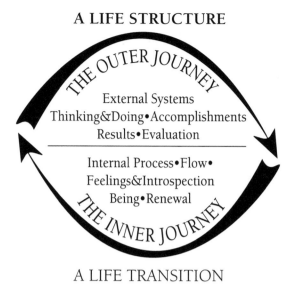

THE OUTER JOURNEY

External Systems
Thinking&Doing•Accomplishments
Results•Evaluation

Internal Process•Flow•
Feelings&Introspection
Being•Renewal

THE INNER JOURNEY

A LIFE TRANSITION

When you're in a transition, at first you feel out of sorts, but in time you become renewed and self-sufficient. Because your interface with the world around you seems tentative, you invest most highly in the world within you. You seek to learn, discover, and grow as a person.

~ This is your *inner journey* into your own identity, self-esteem, and core values.

~ In a transition, you concentrate on refurbishing *your own inner self—the vital center of all renewal.* You awaken to new forces and callings within yourself.

~ You discover *new possibilities for your life ahead.* This is a journey into your own capacity to redirect yourself— with new vision and strength—toward a future that will add meaning to your life. Transitions position you toward the future, with reduced attachment to the past. You are freed to dream again, to take charge of your life, and to redefine the purpose of the next chapter of your life.

~ Transitions also provide you with social rites of passage, to link together the chapters of your life, so you can feel yourself "graduating" from one chapter of life into the next. These help you measure your lifelong journey.

To stay renewed, you need to know how to manage both experiences: building successful external life chap-

A round man cannot be expected to fit in a square hole right away. He must have time to modify his shape.
—Mark Twain

In spite of warnings,
nothing much happens
until the status quo
becomes more painful
than change.
—L. J. Peter

ters and discovering new internal resources through your transitions. Both experiences are natural, desirable, and inevitable parts of the ever-renewing cycle of change.

The Four Phases of Change–
A Renewal Cycle

The basic flow of our lives is a cycle of stable times followed by transitions, throughout our lives. This flow follows *a pattern of four predictable phases:*

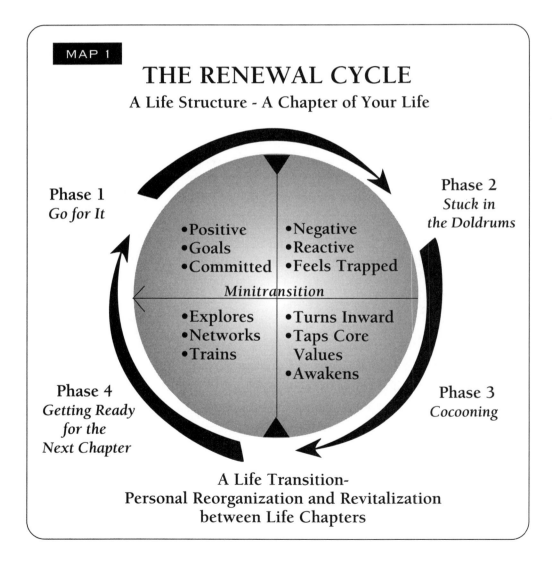

MAP 1

THE RENEWAL CYCLE
A Life Structure - A Chapter of Your Life

Phase 1
Go for It

Phase 2
Stuck in the Doldrums

•Positive
•Goals
•Committed

•Negative
•Reactive
•Feels Trapped

Minitransition

•Explores
•Networks
•Trains

•Turns Inward
•Taps Core Values
•Awakens

Phase 4
Getting Ready for the Next Chapter

Phase 3
Cocooning

A Life Transition-
Personal Reorganization and Revitalization
between Life Chapters

A Life Structure

PHASE 1, "GO FOR IT," is the positive part of a life chapter, when you seek to live your dream and—if all goes well—reach a sustainable plateau of success and well-being. When you're in Phase 1, you feel linear and expansive. You are mostly harmonious, optimistic, and determined. This is the phase that you probably love the most, and you think it's supposed to last forever while getting better and better. NOT. Sooner or later, even if you succeed at reaching your goals, you get flat, out of synch, low on energy, and reactive. What was an unstoppable dream becomes something like a growing nightmare.

The challenges wane, the routines become familiar, and you feel imprisoned by the very scenario you thought would lead to your fulfillment. You are in the "doldrums."

PHASE 2, "STUCK IN THE DOLDRUMS," is a down time, a protracted sense of decline, when you're not happy with your life chapter, but you don't think you can do much about it. It is not merely that you feel stuck, or out of gas. The chapter of life you are in—with all its players and events—seems stuck as well. When you're in Phase 2, the dream fades, your life routines become all too familiar, and there is growing dissonance between you and the other players in your chapter. You feel like you are in a quagmire from which you can't extricate yourself, as if you were wounded, helpless, and without resources to see ahead.

Your life chapter becomes heavy and out of synch. Your motivation decreases, your negativism increases, and you feel trapped in the very settings and activities you thought would fulfill you. You resist change because you don't know what to do to make things better, but in fact you are defensive and prickly much of the time. Unfortunately, adults tend to remain in Phase 2 longer than anywhere else in the cycle, because they feel victimized and immobilized by forces beyond themselves. Even

When we are pla-teaued, we are not so much actively unhappy as we are just not happy. We could continue to live as we are, because usually it's not awful. But it is also not joyous. Most of us do not make changes in our lives until the pain in the present eclipses our fear of the future.
—Judith M. Bardwick

though they complain and whine, they would rather remain unhappy with what they have than risk a new direction. They would rather feel the pain of their declin-ing—but familiar—chapter than take a chance on some unfamiliar new course of action.

The truth is, at this point in the cycle you are not really stuck or trapped. You have two choices: improve the script (if this is possible) and renew your current chapter of life, or end this chapter and begin a transition toward a brand new chapter. Whenever you are mired in the doldrums, stay proactive and choose one of these two paths before you become comfortable with your discomfort.

I have recently and reluctantly come to the conclusion that I am lost. Not just unsure that this is the right trail, but off any trail whatsoever. I find myself, figuratively, looking for footprints, broken twigs, any sign that someone has been over this ground ahead of me.
—Bill Bridges

Mini-Transition

Correct and improve the chapter you are in. Ninety-nine percent of the time, when you fatigue of feeling sorry for yourself in the doldrums of a life chapter, you try to fix the chapter. You do something you believe will correct the problems and get you back on course again. You strive to improve the chapter you are in. You take a short-cut across the Renewal Cycle (see page 54), called a mini-transition.

After all, you've invested a lot of energy and money in creating and sustaining this chapter of your life, so why not put some more effort in reforming it? In effect, you conduct a personal strategic plan, sorting out the assets from the liabilities. You keep the main themes, roles, and characters of your chapter, but you make some significant changes as well—perhaps geographic location, or job, or career, or marital status. Overall, it feels like minor surgery, and in a few weeks or months you are back to Phase 1 with a repaired and renewed continuation of the same chapter of your life. If the mini-transition renews your chapter with resilience, hope, and challenge, you may stay in this chapter for a long time. But if the mini-transition does not produce these qualities, and leaves you disappointed and discouraged, you automatically move on to cocooning.

A Life Transition

PHASE 3, "COCOONING," is a detachment from the chapter that wasn't working, taking emotional "time out" to heal, reflect, and discover new directions for your life, eventually leading to renewal and revitalization. Phase 3 actually begins in the pain of Phase 2 but becomes a full-time preoccupation when you say goodbye to your old life structure. It takes an ending to find a new beginning. Within the "goodbye" is a liberation from the roles and preoccupations that distressed you.

When you cocoon, you take stock of your life, talk to yourself, and get in touch with your core values and feelings. Just as a caterpillar cannot anticipate becoming a butterfly when it enters its cocoon, adults feel awkward and lost at the beginning of a transition, but when they come out of the cocoon they feel transformed with new life direction. You lose control over much of your life, but you gain inner trust and spiritual readiness to grow.

People in Phase 3 are quiet, withdrawn, often emotional, and unsure of themselves. You don't have to stop living or working to cocoon, although the less energy you invest in your various roles, the sooner you are likely to be fed and replenished by your real self. Just as pruning a rose bush leads to a more robust plant, so cocooning enables people to discover new parts of themselves.

To cocoon is to be gifted with new strength and challenging script, from the inside-out. Cocooning has more to do with the regeneration of positive feelings of self-regard and spiritual trust beyond yourself than with "doing" anything. Although cocooning usually takes many months, it leads to a profound inner renewal of energy, purpose, and hope. You end up with new script —the beginning of a new "story" for your next chapter of life.

PHASE 4, "GETTING READY FOR THE NEXT CHAPTER," is a time for experimenting, training, and networking, resulting in a launching of your next chapter. This is like being in school again, preparing for the rest of your life.

The secret of man's being is not only to live but to have something to live for.
—Dostoyevsky

58

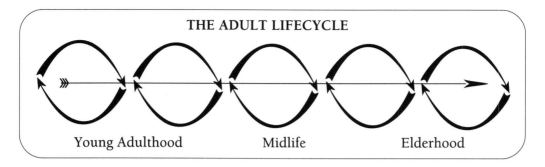

THE ADULT LIFECYCLE

Young Adulthood   Midlife   Elderhood

People in Phase 4 are optimistic, dreamy, confident, creative. They experiment, network, and invest in learning. It's like being in college again. They are very eager to explore new skill sets and ways of thinking. They are also reluctant to make lasting commitments.

They are trying on new roles as possibilities, not moving into long-term decisions. After a few months or so, people in Phase 4 find some path ahead that seems both visionary and practical—a path requiring longer-term commitments. At that point, you write the script for the next chapter of your life and plunge into it, leaving your transition with gratitude and butterfly-like wings. You also have a touch of sadness, because you leave the freedom of Phase 4 for the responsibilities of Phase 1.

The continuous flow of the four phases is how we grow and develop throughout our adult years. That's what makes it the renewal cycle. It's something like a river moving along through all kinds of weather, through all the seasons, through all kinds of terrain and environments. Each complete cycle has two parts, with the life structure being the themes and activities you knit together as a chapter of your life, and the transition being an unraveling — a letting go followed by the discovery of new themes and activities that you want for the next chapter of your life. And on and on it goes throughout our years.*

Stephen and Susan

The lives of Stephen and Susan reveal the dynamics of both parts of the renewing cycle of change. They have

* If you want further insight into the renewal cycle and how to apply it to your life, read **The Adult Years: Mastering the Art of Self-Renewal**, by Frederic Hudson [San Francisco: Jossey-Bass, 1999.]

been married for nineteen years. With three children, they have lived in four different locations across the United States as Stephen climbed the ladder of his career. Although each move felt like a tidal wave to Susan, who hated to leave friends and school systems, Stephen strongly felt that the number one priority was reaching his peak, so the family could benefit from financial security and stability. That's not the way it worked out.

Before Stephen was six months into his fourth management job, in Chicago, he was summarily fired. His superiors accused him of being autocratic, ego driven, lacking in empathy and listening skills, and fundamentally unable to collaborate with his workforce. Stephen was suddenly unemployed—he was crushed on the inside, and enraged. Although he immediately tried to locate new management positions, no one seemed interested in him. His seething temperament and overeager style got him nowhere in the job interviews he landed.

That was only the beginning of the bottom falling out of his life. Now that Stephen's career was disrailed, Susan insisted on evaluating their marriage and family life. "I can't take it any more," she said. "We haven't seen much of you, Stephen, for over a decade. You just work, work, work. And then we move so you can work some more. I know we need money, but I won't live this way any more. Betty is now sixteen, and she's been off track for over three years—seriously. She barely knows who you are. Jimmy is thirteen and so much wants to be close to you, but you're never here—and when you are, we all know you're just getting rested so you can get back to work. I've got a part-time job, but I also manage the home and family, and I just won't do it alone any more."

Stephen was at the end of a chapter of his life. When he was younger, he had designed his work roles and career path to fit his life as a twenty-year-old. He defined his life through his work as his father had done. But now the messages from his employer, wife and children, along with his inner anger and outmoded management style add up to time for a life transition.

. . . .

He took time off to reevaluate things, and in the process he learned a lot about himself and his preferred life direction. He went on some long trips with his children, and got closer to their concerns and hurts. He and Susan joined a couple's group to look at ways to grow their marriage. He even came to wonder why he had spent so many years trying to be someone he never really was. At home, he and his son Jimmy built a new addition onto his house.

Stephen developed daily rituals—going on walks, meeting friends at the spa, cooking meals, and planning weekend getaways. He also became involved at his church with the family camping programs. Meanwhile, Susan invested more time in her work, both to develop her career further and to provide necessary funding for the transition.

Little by little, Stephen caught up with his own depth and breadth. He found a job near his home that paid fairly well, although not nearly as much as the career track he had been on. But his new work engaged him in team work, with ongoing training, and balanced well with his new roles in the family. When his transition ended, Stephen had new script, a new story, and a life plan that deepened his journey as a human being by reevaluating his priorities, time commitments, and roles. He and his family were on their way again.

The Magic Formula

Knowing how to move yourself around the cycle of renewing change is like staying in shape; it empowers you to be at your best at all times, whether you are assuming leadership roles while structuring, or shedding those roles because they have become stale habits, or unavailable, in a transition.

There is a magic formula of eight words that will keep this map close to you: **Hold on, Let go, Take on, Move on**. As you consider your best choices for composing your life, sort out each option into one of these categories:

Hold on to what is valuable in you and in your connections to the world around you. Hold on to what is working in your life. Don't ever trash everything. There is always something precious and gem-like to take with you and to build upon in the journey ahead. The older you are, the greater your reservoir of experience for finding diamonds and rubies. Always hold on to what you value in yourself and your relationships before you do anything else.

Let go of what's not working, of what is worn out, of what doesn't belong to your future. In our society it is practically un-American to let go of anything you accumulate, from things to habits, but letting go of what is dysfunctional in you and your human settings is a prerequisite to taking on healthy options for the future. You can't truly take on new directions until you let go of the excess baggage in your life. Just as a snake must shed its skin to grow a new one, you have to risk letting go to gain freedom for moving on into new possibilities.

Take on new skills, attitudes, and resources for creating the next chapter of your life. Taking on involves learning, training, growing, and becoming. It is an invitation to awaken to more of yourself and to take advantage of the world as a veritable campus awaiting your self-directed study program. Learn to evolve!

Move on is what happens when you hold on, let go, and take on. New paths appear. Your sail feels the wind as your rudder guides you to new destinations. You feel yourself on a new pilgrimage you believe in. You find yourself at a new beginning—fresh, ready, and eager. You are on your way.

And this too will end, as the cycle of renewing change goes on and on.

Your Turn!

1. Are you at several places on the renewal cycle, with parts of you active to launching, while other parts are complaining? Your various roles will always be spread around the cycle, but you, yourself, the conscious center

of the person that is living your life, are at one place in the cycle. Write down in your notebook where you think you are in your various roles, such as spouse, worker, parent, friend and community leader, etc. Then indicate the approximate place you are as a whole person or self, at this time in your life. You can tell your central place in the renewal cycle by your feelings and the life tasks that engage you.

2. Which of the four steps of the renewal cycle are you most familiar and comfortable with (Go for It, Stuck in the Doldrums, Cocooning, or Getting Ready for the Next Chapter)? Least familiar with? What you would like that you don't now know?

3. Leaving home in your teens or twenties to begin the adult years is your first adult transition. Describe your experience below:
~ What was your cocooning like when you left home? Where were you, what were you doing, and what were you feeling?
~ When you began to explore possibilities for launching the first chapter of your adult life, what were your options and considerations, and how did you get ready for making it successful?
~ Who were the primary characters in the first chapter of your adult life?
~ What was your vision or dream for that first chapter of adult life, and what action plans did you follow to live your dream?
~ What did you learn from leaving home—your first adult transition?

4. Some people have trouble seeing a transition as a positive force in their life. What words do you associate with a "transition?" What *positive developments* might accompany disruptive events like the following?
~ A friend finds herself jobless after fifteen years in a corporate setting.

~ A colleague decides to leave the rat race to live on less.
~ You win the lottery.
~ A close friend leaves his or her marriage.
~ Your mother suffers a stroke.
~ You give birth to your first child and all of your old notions about work and goals seem irrelevant.

5. What is *a successful* transition, for you? Have you ever had one? If so, describe the characteristics in your experience that made it successful.

6. Describe the finest chapter in your life thus far. What makes it "the finest"? How can you have these qualities in your next life structure?

CHAPTER 5

MAP 2
A Deliberate Life
Living with Passion and Purpose

. . . .

Map 1 helped you locate where you are in the adult territory—managing the tentative stability of a life structure or swimming in the flow of transitional change in search of new directions for your life. Knitting together or unravelling and then beginning again. The adult years are a steady journey around this cycle and if you know where you are, at any time, in your heart of hearts, you will know how to proceed ahead, what to look forward to, and which life skills to utilize.

Map 2 will help you locate your deep energy and passion for the destinations you now want to pursue. Yesterday's passions may not serve tomorrow's goals, so ask yourself "what motivates me the most at this time in my life to be the best I can be?" That's the fuel for your next LifeLaunch.

We do not need to run out of gas in midlife. More often we fail to use the variety of fuels available to us. There are several sources of passion within us, and as we move through the adult life cycle, we usually shift to new sources of energy.

Getting in Touch with Your Current Passions and Values

What you want for your life at forty is seldom what you wanted at twenty, and at sixty or eighty you have yet different passions and goals. To a greater or lesser degree, your priorities change.

After examining hundreds of biographies of twentieth century successful adults, we found that the persons we examined measured their lives with six different basic values or passions—often in combination with one another. These six core values compete for our loyalty and passionate commitment throughout the life course, and we often shift gears throughout the adult years from familiar, accomplished passion areas to less familiar, attractive, and energizing values:

~ **Personal Mastery**—*Know Thyself*
~ **Achievement**—*Reach Your Goals*

~ Intimacy—*Love and Be Loved*
~ Play and Creativity—*Follow Your Intuition*
~ Search for Meaning—*Spiritual Integrity*
~ Compassion and Contribution—*Leave a Legacy*

Each of these draws upon a different source of our human energy, but every adult has the capacity to tap all six passions, in various combinations, at various times in the lifecycle, to sustain vitality and purpose. Too often we lock ourselves into the passions and values of our young adult years, and burn out during midlife, losing our passion for life. A better approach is to keep evaluating your priorities and preferences, to be sure that at any time in your life you are marching to your own drumbeats, empowered by the values you most honor at that time in your life.

Your passions are your internal energy source, the fire or determination you have for reaching some destination up ahead. They tell you why you are on this journey and what you want from life. They are your push and your pull. Find your passion for living this chapter of your life—and make it happen!

Until you make peace with who you are, you'll never be content with what you have.
—Doris Mortman

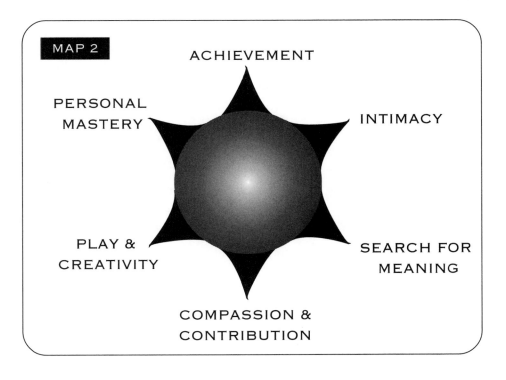

MAP 2

ACHIEVEMENT

PERSONAL MASTERY

INTIMACY

PLAY & CREATIVITY

SEARCH FOR MEANING

COMPASSION & CONTRIBUTION

The Six Adult Passions

Each life structure during your adult years has a different value base from previous ones. Your priorities change. Your expectations shift, particularly during life transitions. You create new preferences and ways to spend your time.

Most life chapters are built upon three or four of these passions. How would you rank order these six in relationship to the next chapter of your life? First read this entire section so you have a good grasp of all six passions and how they function. Then indicate in your journal or notebook how you would rank-order (1-6) the passions for the next chapter of your life. Let 1 be the most important and 6 the least important, for the emerging chapter of your life. Then concentrate on how you would engage in your next chapter with your top three or four passions. The doors to your future will open, and your energy will flow ahead.

PERSONAL MASTERY: *Claiming Yourself*
Self-esteem, confidence, identity, inner motivation, a positive sense of self, clear ego boundaries, self-love, courage.
Ways to increase personal power:
~ Stay around people who sustain their resilience
~ Take good care of your body
~ Be assertive and clear
~ Test your leadership abilities
~ Hang out with healthy people
~ Balance the parts of your life
~ Network actively through strategic alliances
~ Stay commited to your personal goals
~ Read works by Hugh Prather, Jeffrey Kottler, Ellen Goodman, Daniel Goleman, Anna Quindlen, Anthony Storr, Jean Baker Miller, Rosalind Barnett, Carol Gilligan

Never doubt that a small group of thoughtful, committed citizens can change the world. Indeed, it is the only thing that ever has.
—Margaret Mead

ACHIEVEMENT: Proving Yourself

Reaching goals, conducting projects, working, winning, playing in organized sports, having ambition, getting results and recognition and $, being purposive, doing.

Ways to pursue achievement:
- ~ Maintain clear goals and objectives
- ~ Use time-management planning
- ~ Connect to friends who are winners
- ~ Join network groups in your goal areas
- ~ Stay in training
- ~ Evaluate frequently
- ~ Read writings of Charles Garfield, Rosabeth Moss Kanter, Stephen R. Covey, Tom Peters, Warren Bennis

Winning is not everything, but it is something powerful, indeed beautiful, in itself, something as necessary to the strong spirit as striving is necessary to the healthy character.
—A. Bartlett Giamatti

INTIMACY: Sharing Yourself

Loving, bonding, caring, being intimate, making relationships work, touching, feeling close, nesting, coupling, parenting, being a friend.

Ways to increase intimacy:
- ~ Speak from the heart
- ~ Be a friend
- ~ Seek fairness
- ~ Be open to new ways
- ~ Offer intimacy and risk rejection
- ~ Touch
- ~ Avoid blame
- ~ Face conflict and seek solutions
- ~ Ritualize—phone, flowers, celebrations
- ~ Speak the truth
- ~ Read writings of Elizabeth B. Browning, Sam Keen, Sam Osherson, Harville Hendrix

Without love the acquisition of knowledge only increases confusion and leads to self-destruction.
—Krishnamurti

PLAY AND CREATIVITY: Expressing Yourself

Being imaginative, intuitive, playful, spontaneous, original, expressive, humorous, artistic, celebrative, re-creative, funny, curious, childlike, and non-purposive.

Ways to pursue play and creativity:

- ~ Follow your feelings
- ~ Learn simple ways to express yourself
- ~ Walk the beach or a forest path
- ~ Play with children
- ~ Fly kites
- ~ Be a clown
- ~ Buy yourself some toys
- ~ Play with clay
- ~ Shout and laugh in your car
- ~ Sing daily
- ~ Get some fun friends
- ~ Read the writings on creativity by Silvano Arieti, Julia Cameron, Robert Grundin, Willis Harman, Madeleine L'Engle, Roger von Oech, and George Prince

Man is most nearly himself when he achieves the seriousness of a child at play.
—Heraclitus

SEARCH FOR MEANING: Integrating Yourself

Finding wholeness, unity, integrity, peace, an inner connection to all things, spirituality, trust in the flow of life, inner wisdom, a sense of transcendence, bliss.

Ways to pursue search for meaning:

- ~ Meditate daily in silence
- ~ Introspect—look within yourself
- ~ Pray—no matter what you believe
- ~ Listen to your inner self
- ~ Walk alone in nature
- ~ Go on a vision quest
- ~ Take long drives, alone.
- ~ Seek out wise elders
- ~ Learn your family history and roots
- ~ Be a mentor
- ~ Read biographies
- ~ Listen to music

It is only by living completely in this world that one learns to have faith.
—Dietrich Bonhoeffer

~ Embark on faith-centered therapy
~ Read the works of Anne Morrow Lindbergh, Victor Frankl, Arthur Ashe, M. Scott Peck, Eugene Bianchi, Charlotte Buhler, Gloria Steinem, Thomas More, and Ram Dass

COMPASSION & CONTRIBUTION: *Giving Yourself*
Improving, helping, feeding, reforming, leaving the world a better place, bequeathing, being generative, serving, social and environmental caring, institution-building, volunteerism.

Ways to pursue compassion and contribution:
~ Do a good deed, anonymously
~ Meditate on compassion and contribution
~ Practice dying
~ Replace acquisition with divestiture
~ Support your favorite cause, actively
~ Work with the homeless in your town
~ Join the Habitat for Humanity
~ Pursue peace at every level of your life
~ Read the works of Sister Theresa, Albert Schweitzer, Eleanor D. Roosevelt, Martin Luther King, Jimmy Carter, Mortimer J. Adler, Marian Wright Edelman, John Gardner, Robert Bellah, Ken Keyes, Betty Friedan, Peter Block, Nelson Mandela, and Bill Moyers

I don't know what your destiny will be, but one thing I know: the only ones among you who will be really happy are those who have sought and found how to serve.
—Albert Schweitzer

Passionate Destinations

Your values are your compass for guiding your journey into your next LifeLaunch. They will point you toward what matters most to you. What are some of the passionate destinations you want to get from your passions at this time in your life? How do you want your next chapter to come out? What will the results be? Take your top three or four passions that you want to direct your next chapter of life and construct a script for the next chapter of your life, keeping you at the growth-edge of your human development.

Example: I want to form three deep and long-lasting friendships in the next two years with my "intimacy," and I want to become an active leader in my local Hospice with my "compassion and contribution," and I want to complete an MBA with my "achievement" so I can move into upper management within the next five years.

Write out, for yourself, in your journal or notebook, some of the compelling results you want from your passions in the next chapter of your life.

How Do You Count What Counts?

What are your measuring sticks, your private ways of counting your success through life? Money? Position? Acquisitions? Status? Power? Authority? Career Success? Ability to Help Others? Loving? Parenting? Friendships? Sexual Prowess? Travel? Integrity? Caring Influence? Spirituality?

Choose your top five items from the following list. What are your measuring sticks for the next chapter of your life, in the next few years?

It is better to follow the Voice inside and be at war with the whole world, than to follow the ways of the world and be at war with your deepest self.
—Michael Pastore

~ The accumulation of money and things.
~ Being validated and respected by others for your accomplishments.
~ Being in love and sustaining deep intimacy, incluing friendships.
~ Parenting your children.
~ Being effective and successful at work.
~ Having fun, and investing highly in your favorite pastimes, hobbies or sports activities.
~ Following your beliefs, your spiritual path.
~ Joining causes you believe in, to make a lasting contribution.
~ Others:

What is Your Life Purpose, Today?

Whenever you consult your life's compass within you, it points toward the current purpose of your life. Your values, deep energy, and passionate destinations are all wrapped up into one profound sense of purpose, pulling you ahead into more of yourself, through the chapters of your life. That sense of purpose is like a vibrant channel, an illuminated path, a personal calling.

Your emerging purpose is more than a set of goals. It is your compelling reason for being alive. It is your raison d'etre, your personal/social version of inalienable rights. It is a pursuit of excellence beyond your reach, a sense of manifest destiny, an unstoppable drive.

It measures an era of your life by defining your central themes, context, and basic beliefs. It is essential, if adults are to be alive in a world of flux and complexity that they have within themselves a clear sense of purpose—to measure the flow of external change by the abiding values of internal meaning.

"Life shrinks or expands in proportion to one's courage."
—Anais Nin

In your notebook, write out a statement of purpose for the next chapter of your life. Keep your statement simple, succinct, poetic, and empowering. It can connect your top three or four passions to destinations you want to travel toward in your next chapter.

Begin with this phrase: *"My purpose, for the next chapter of my life, is to …."*

CHAPTER 6

MAP 3

Life's Assignments

Balancing the Parts of Your Life:
Activities - Roles - Commitments

In **Map 1**, you learned the pattern of renewal and how to manage yourself proactively throughout the cycle of change.

In **Map 2**, you identified your primary values and passions, so you can empower yourself through the next chapter of your life with a sense of purpose.

In Map 3, you are invited to explore your most important adult roles for empowering the next chapter of your life.

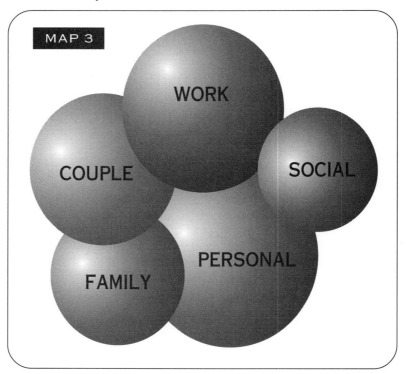

Map 3 suggests that most adults distribute their time in five directions:

1. Personal activities and roles
2. Couple activities and roles
3. Family/Friends activities
4. Work activities and roles
5. Social connection activities and roles

I will speak of the whole.
—Democritus

The task of Map 3 is to define, as precisely as possible, how you will schedule yourself—by intent and design—into specific activities and roles that represent, at this time in your life, what your passion and purpose are about. Conversely, the task is to define, as precisely as possible, what activities and roles in your current schedule need to be reduced or eliminated if you are going to live with inner and outer integrity.

If you could connect the passion and purpose you've distilled from Map 2 to the select, strategic activities that would fulfill you in the next chapter of your life—what would those activities be? Remember, what counts is not the quantity of activities but the quality links among your emerging passions, sense of purpose, and strategic activities.

Define Your Activities and Roles

Everybody has roles—things you do over and over, in certain settings—as a worker, commuter, or cook, for example. Adults have many roles.

Just as fish cannot live without water to swim in, you cannot live without meaningful roles in the world around you—in families, careers, work organizations, friendship associations, electronic systems, civic and professional groups, and communities. The problem is that over the years, many of your roles do not remain as meaningful and fulfilling as they used to be, while others grow to be more promising than ever. It is up to you to alter and retool your roles. As you think about your next chapter, it is very important to get perspective on how which activities and roles will work best for you.

In your notebook, make a threefold evaluation of which of your current activities:

1. Essential: Which activities are essential and necessary for you at this time in your life, whether you like them or not. How can you make them as constructive and fulfilling as possible?

2. Fulfilling: Which activities are fulfilling for you at this time of your life—the ones you prefer and like the best? How can you invest more time in these and deepen the positive activities of your life?

3. Unfulfilling: Which activities are unrewarding or even punishing at this time of your life? How can you invest less time in these, and minimize their impact on your life course?

To be nobody-but-yourself—in a world which is doing its best, night and day, to make you everybody else— means to fight the hardest battle which any human being can fight; and never stop fighting.
—e. e. cummings

Map 3 has five areas within which we carve out activities for ourselves, or have them assigned to us: personal activities, couple activities, family activities, work activities, and social connections. Within those activities listed below, identify activities you will include in your immediate future and record them in your notebook with any personal observations you may have.

1. PERSONAL ACTIVITIES AND ROLES—For the care and feeding of yourself

Your personal activities connect you to the basic system of your life, to all the others that matter to you. You act as your own best friend, a major source of affirmation, and your best critic. Invest highly in this area, but not to the exclusion of others. In this role, the prime effort is to sustain and enrich such matters as:

~ *Use of personal space and areas*
~ *Nutrition and exercise*
~ *Personal friends*
~ *Managing priorities*
~ *Personal time, alone*
~ *Personal nurturing and self-care*
~ *Personal spirituality*
~ *Budgeting and managing money*
~ *Training for personal growth*
~ *Others*

In your journal or workbook, organize your personal activities for the next few years in three categories:

1. Essential: Those activities that are necessary for you at this time in your life, whether you like them or not. In the next chapter of your life, how can you effectively maintain your essential personal activities?

2. Fulfilling: Those activities that are fulfilling for you at this time of your life. In the next chapter of your life, how can you increase your investment in your fulfilling personal activities?

3. Unfulfilling: Those activities that are unrewarding or even punishing at this time of your life. In the next chapter of your life, how can you eliminate or at least diminish your unfulfilling personal activities?

2. COUPLE ACTIVITIES AND ROLES—The nurture, fun, intimate contact, and management of conflict you have with a significant other or best friend

None of us gets much personal training in "coupling," yet these adult activities often weave through most of the others where we share our most intimate concerns as lover, friend, and advocate. Which of the following fit your coupling activities for the next few years:

~ *Talking and touching*
~ *Shared roles, tasks, and fun*
~ *Shared projects and activities outside the home*
~ *Separate projects and activities outside the home*
~ *Managing priorities*
~ *Managing conflicts*
~ *Intimacy and sex*
~ *Couple friendships*
~ *Interfacing with each other's work commitments*
~ *Management of shared health needs*
~ *Budgeting and managing money*
~ *Recreation and leisure activities, including TV*
~ *Adventuring, learning, and traveling together*
~ *Other*

In your journal or workbook, organize your evolving couple activities in three categories:

1. Essential: Those activities that are necessary for you at this time in your life, whether you like them or not. In the next chapter of your life, how can you effectively maintain your essential couple activities?

2. Fulfilling: Those activities that are fulfilling for you at this time of your life. In the next chapter of your life, how can you increase your investment in your fulfilling couple activities?

3. Unfulfilling: Those activities that are unrewarding or even punishing at this time of your life. In the next chapter of your life, how can you eliminate or at least diminish your unfulfilling couple activities?

The good news is that sometimes the bond between a husband and wife is stronger than any damage that can be done to it. The bad news is that no two adults can do each other more damage than husband and wife.
—Judith Viorst

I looked on child rearing not only as a work of love and duty but as a profession that was fully as interesting and challenging as any honorable profession in the world, and one that demanded the best that I could bring to it.
—Rose Kennedy

3. FAMILY/FRIENDSHIP ACTIVITIES AND ROLES— The extended intimate relationships and responsibilities that come with caring for children, parents, and close friends

The activities that attend managing family system and friendship networks are complex and varied. Parenting alone is a very demanding role, requiring deep devotion, caring, leadership, time, and patience. Yet parenting activities change as children grow up. Many adults spend more time caring for their aging parents than they spent raising their own children. Networking with friends is an important supplement to family ties. Choose from among the following those which are part of your family system activities for the next few years:

~ *Parenting*
~ *Cooking/eating*
~ *TV and movie monitoring*
~ *Maintaining a home*
~ *Education of children*
~ *Enjoying vacations*
~ *Management of health needs*
~ *Management of money*
~ *Sports activities and hobbies*
~ *Family friends*
~ *Spiritual development*
~ *Caring for parents*
~ *Nurturing extended family*
~ *At home learning, lessons, help*
~ *Traveling with friends*

In your journal or workbook, organize your family activities in three categories:

1. Essential: Those activities that are necessary for you at this time in your life, whether you like them or not. In the next chapter of your life, how can you effectively maintain your essential family/friends activities?

2. Fulfilling: Those activities that are fulfilling for you at this time of your life. In the next chapter of your life, how can you increase your investment in your fulfilling family/friends activities?

3. Unfulfilling: Those activities that are unrewarding or even punishing at this time of your life. In the next chapter of your life, how can you eliminate or at least diminish your unfulfilling family/friends activities?

4. WORK ACTIVITIES AND ROLES—Your job, career, or volunteer efforts to make a living or to find meaning within a work system

Most adults spend more time in their work activities than in any others. Work roles involve much more than a job description. Think about it. You have "work groups" demanding fairly high levels of interpersonal and decision-making skills. You have relationships with "authorities," with friends; and with continuous goal setting, time management, and achieved results. You work for many reasons, and those reasons keep shifting over the years: to acquire a necessary funding mechanism; to complete a lap in your career; to make social contact and to have fun; to be challenged and to get rewarded; to lead and make important contributions; to acquire necessary benefits for health and retirement; to volunteer because of causes and groups you believe in.

What are your current work activities, and what are your primary reasons for working at this time in your life? Choose from among the following those items which you want to belong to your work activities during the next few years:

~ *Commuting or not commuting*
~ *Completing work assignments effectively*
~ *Career training*
~ *Weekend assignments*
~ *Work friends*
~ *Social activities*
~ *Volunteer commitments*
~ *Leadership*
~ *Supervising others*
~ *Waiting for the right time to change jobs/careers*
~ *Management*

Many a businessman feels himself the prisoner of the commodities he sells; he has a feeling of fraudulency about this project and a secret contempt for it. Most important of all, he hates himself, because he sees his life passing him by without making any sense beyond the momentary intoxication of success.
—Erich Fromm

~ *Getting results*
~ *Necessary career step*
~ *Retirement planning*
~ *Nurturing creative projects*
~ *Other*

In your journal or workbook, organize your work activities in three categories:

1. Essential: Those activities that are necessary for you at this time in your life, whether you like them or not. In the next chapter of your life, how can you effectively maintain your essential work activities?

2. Fulfilling: Those activities that are fulfilling for you at this time of your life. In the next chapter of your life, how can you increase your investment in your fulfilling work activities?

3. Unfulfilling: Those activities that are unrewarding or even punishing at this time of your life. In the next chapter of your life, how can you eliminate or at least diminish your unfulfilling work activities?

5. SOCIAL CONNECTIONS—Your involvement in community organizations and activities

None of us would have functional lives if it were not for a broad-based society that sustained sufficient order and meaning for our personal and family lives. At some point in the adult journey, most of us find some way to contribute back to the broader swim of things—to serve on boards, to make financial contributions, to support causes, to become politically active, to make a difference. Choose from among the following those items which are part of your emerging activities in the broader society during the next few years:

~ *Participation in community groups*
~ *Membership in professional organizations*
~ *Commitment to neighborhood*
~ *Participation in religious institutions*

Our task must be to free ourselves from this prison by widening our circle of compassion to embrace all living creatures, and the whole of nature in its beauty.
—Albert Einstein

~ *Participation in social causes and political groups*
~ *Participation in environmental concerns*
~ *Volunteer activities in the community*
~ *Taking adult education courses or getting an advanced degree*
~ *Participation in network groups, including electronic networks*
~ *Other*

In your journal or workbook, organize your social **activities** in three categories:

1. *Essential:* Those activities that are necessary for you at this time in your life, whether you like them or not. In the next chapter of your life, how can you effectively maintain your essential social connection activities?

2. *Fulfilling:* Those activities that are fulfilling for you at this time of your life. In the next chapter of your life, how can you increase your investment in your fulfilling social connection activities?

3. *Unfulfilling:* Those activities that are unrewarding or even punishing at this time of your life. In the next chapter of your life, how can you eliminate or at least diminish your unfulfilling social activities?

How Do You Balance Your Activities and Roles?

Many adults suffer because they don't know how to manage and balance their evolving activities and roles. They feel like they are drowning in the very activities they wanted to swim in.

To achieve balance, become a master at time management, and be sure to give adequate time to your essential and fulfilling activities, while keeping your unfulfilling activities carefully boundaried.

To a large degree, you are the way you spend your time, and the roles within which you spend your time shape your behavior, concerns and outlook. The following experiment asks you to do two things: first, to discover

I'm working all day and I'm working all night
To be good-looking, healthy, and wise.
And adored, contented, brave, and well-read.
And a marvelous hostess, fantastic in bed.
And bilingual, athletic, artistic—
Won't someone please stop me?
—Judith Viorst

Example:

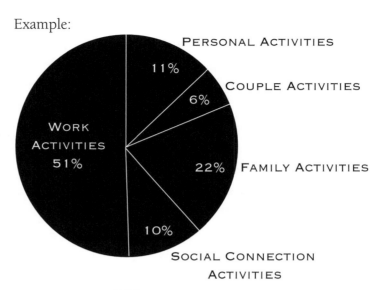

WORK ACTIVITIES 51%

PERSONAL ACTIVITIES 11%

COUPLE ACTIVITIES 6%

FAMILY ACTIVITIES 22%

SOCIAL CONNECTION ACTIVITIES 10%

A human being is part of the whole, called by us 'Universe'; a part limited in time and space. He experiences himself, his thoughts, and feelings as something separated from the rest — a kind of optical delusion of his consciousness. This delusion is a kind of prison for us, restricting us to our personal desires and to affection for a few persons nearest to us.
—Albert Einstein

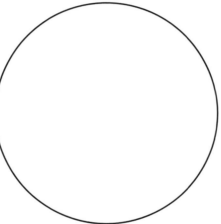

Your Activity Commitments Today

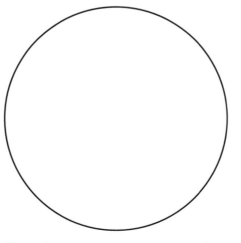

Your Activity Commitments In the
Next Chapter of Your Life

how much time you are now giving to each of your roles; and second, to calculate how much time you want to give to each of those roles during the next chapter of your life.

Instructions: *Using the five areas of activities just reviewed—personal, couple, family, work, and social—conduct an inventory of how much time you currently spend in each area, and how much time you want to spend in those same areas during the next few years. Include weekday and weekend events, excluding sleep. Assume you are awake and involved for* **100 hours per week.**

1. First make a list of how you spend your time in the current chapter of your life, using the formula of 100 hours of waking time per week to spread among your current activities and roles. Use percentages and be sure they add up to 100%.

2. Then make a second list for how you want to invest your time in preferred activities and roles in the forthcoming chapter of your life.

3. When you are done with these approximate mathematical measures of your commitments, transfer them to the two circles (pies) below, assuming that each circle equals 100 hours, and each quarter circle is equivalent to 25 hours. Let each percentage become a slice of pie within a circle.

Man did not weave the web of life, he is merely a strand in it. Whatever he does to the web, he does to himself.
—Chief Seattle

Your Commitments in the Next Chapter of Your Life

Adult change is every bit as social as it is personal. Too often adults think they can individually change their lives, irrespective of the activities and roles they have. **In fact, change is more of a dialogue between you and your social scheduling than anything else.** Gradually, you can increase or diminish your investment in any activity or role, but any change will involve some other role. You trade off one for another, or reduced time-commitments here for increased time-commitments there. Effective adults know how to honor, manipulate, shape, respect, and accept the complex time commitments that their lives represent. Are you ready to do that in your next LifeLaunch?

Your Turn!

1. Which activities and roles are most important, at this time in your life, for living your chosen passion and purpose? List your top three passions from Map 2 for your next chapter, and relate them to those activities and roles that can give them the life forms you are seeking.

2. What is your favorite role—the one in which you are most comfortable and competent? Homemaker? Careerist? Parent? Other? How can you develop similar comfort and competence in the other activities and roles important to you?

3. Your activities and work roles are probably very important to you, right? Then stay on the cutting edge of your work opportunities in your LifeLaunch. When did you last update your résumé? We suggest you revise your résumé at least twice a year, and use specific dates that are noted in your time management system, such as April 1 (should bring on a smile) and Labor Day (yo ho, heave ho). Even if you're not planning on getting a new job, you need to keep etching your new accomplishments into the résumé —including confirming assessments made by your clients and internal evaluators—so you're always ready to promote your work future, if and when you need to or want to. Every update of your résumé will help you to discern the career path you are creating for yourself.

4. For many adults, their "couple" activities are the least nurtured. You can revive and redefine your couple roles. Commit two weekends about six months apart for the renewal of your "couple" relationship—not just a nice time away, but time to consciously rewrite a couple's mission statement, or to create a priorities list for the coming year. Keep this relationship on the edge of tomorrow, not yesterday.

CHAPTER 7

MAP 4
The Grand Adventure
From Twenty to Ninety

. . . .

Map 4 describes the general themes, issues, and callings of adults throughout the lifecycle. It portrays the vast variety of LifeLaunches, from about age 20 to age 90 or so. This map will help you plan "developmentally," with foresight into optimal life choices on the path ahead of you. You will learn how to take advantage of whatever age you are.

The Adult Lifecycle

We all walk backward through time, measuring tomorrow by yesterday's familiar scenes. Thoughts about "getting older" usually are accompanied by ignorance and apprehension.

We worry more about not being as young as we were yesterday than about making the most of the next lap ahead of us. We make "young " the ideal, the norm, and "old" a Darth Vader of our mind's eye. Few imagine they can deepen the human journey as they get older, despite overwhelming evidence that they can. The challenge of this chapter is to convey how our lives get older and more resilient, even as our bodies slow down and look different. The smart person looks for advantages in the years ahead and how to maximize them.

Each new LifeLaunch of your adult years feels like a different adventure, guided by shifting concerns and opportunities. What seems all important in your twenties gets replaced by new challenges and callings in midlife and beyond.

Each trip around the never-ending renewal cycle (Map 1) taps different passions and values (Map 2) that lead you to a new balance of activities and roles (Map 3)—providing you a new lease on life (Map 4). This is the basis for growing creatively throughout the life cycle.

The true measure of your journey through the adult years is not your age. Life is not about staying young and not about getting old. The true measure of your life is where you are in relation to becoming complete as a person. Each time you recycle yourself you attend to some area of growth and discovery. True maturity is based

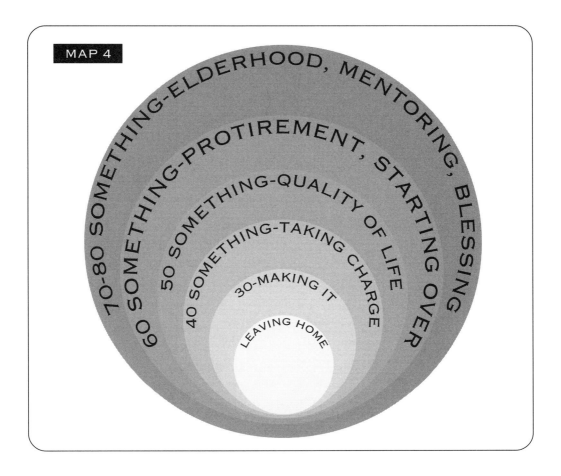

MAP 4

70-80 SOMETHING-ELDERHOOD, MENTORING, BLESSING

60 SOMETHING-PROTIREMENT, STARTING OVER

50 SOMETHING-QUALITY OF LIFE

40 SOMETHING-TAKING CHARGE

30-MAKING IT

LEAVING HOME

upon what you have learned from your life experience, not a reflection of your chronological age.

Life is a series of trade-offs, with some parts of you becoming more present and competent while other parts become less present and competent. Some parts of your life lose importance during the lifecycle while other parts gain importance. Getting older is not about getting worse or better; it's about getting different. Some parts of your life may be less glorious while other parts become bolder and clearer.

On the whole, your physical strengths and attributes gradually decline while your inner, spiritual strengths incline. But even that is too simple. We each change in different ways, at different times in life, for many reasons. Pay most attention to YOUR issues, priorities, and concerns at this time as you formulate the next chapter of your life. There are no firm rules to follow, no predictable stages to enter, no reason to conform to age stereotypes. Just plan your life and live it, your way, no matter what your age.

Even though the rest of this chapter relates developmental issues to decade ages, it is merely a report of current information about age groups in America than a prescription for you to follow. This chapter describes a general flow that actually proceeds differently for each one of us.

The more you know about the range of options in front of you, the less you will fear them, deny them, or fail to thrive on them. The more you know them, the more likely you will choose your path ahead with enthusiasm, as you did when you were younger. This map describes some of the possibilities for your consideration as you compose your life throughout the years.

This life is a test.
It is only a test.
If this had been
a real life,
you would have
been given
instructions
on where to go
and what to do.
—Anonymous Fax

Changing and Abiding Themes

Each adult decade—more or less—represents a complete trip around the renewal cycle, with a life structure followed by a minitransition or a life transition. Map 4 will help you locate where you are in the long haul of your life.

Although you can never be sure how you will feel and think about life a decade from now, there is plenty of information available to help you plan ahead. To begin with:

~ Demystify the cultural myth that getting older means your life is in steady decline.

~ Adopt a "growth model" for your life, so you can envision yourself growing into your fullness as you mature, always finding some way to add value to life.

~ Get specific information on the decades ahead of you so you can anticipate approximate options for making vital future plans. Get yourself beyond fear and denial so you can weave the tapestry of your life with accurate data.

~ Find someone of the same gender who is about ten years older than you and is—to you—a very alive and attractive person, someone you admire. Ask that person to share with you what it feels like to be older, and what the trade-offs are. Get a visceral feel for the journey ahead. You will probably laugh a lot.

~ Maintain a mental picture of how you think your life will be ten years from now, and commit yourself to growing into that person, with expectancy:

— What will be your central activities?

— Who will your friends be?

— Where will you be in your career and work commitments?

— What will your leisure life be like?

— What will your love life and special relation-ships be about?

— What will be your contributions to life around you?

— How will you spend your time?

When you were a child, people probably asked you, "What are you going to do when you grow up?" And you probably dreamed of great things you might become, and strived to make them come true. That is exactly what you need to do today, as you look ahead to your next chapter, because **you never grow up, you just keep growing— on and on and on.**

TWENTYSOMETHING—
Staking Out the Adult World, 18-28

The first chapter of adult life happens when you leave your family of origin and begin to care for yourself. This is an experimental period lasting from late adolescence until about age 28, in which you try on adulthood as if it were an infinite wardrobe of possibilities.

You live out the expectations others had for your life, particularly those of your parents, siblings, teachers, peers, and childhood heroes. Twentysomethings also live out rebellion against those very expectations. You are sensitive to peer opinions and tend to be other-directed, not inner-directed.

If you're a twentysomething, you probably identify your life through your relationships, jobs, and other commitments. You are more sure of "what" you do than "who" you are, at your core. Twentysomethings look at adult life as an experiment they are not fully into, but in fact, they are well on their way.

How to Maximize Your Twenties—

~ *Concentrate on defining yourself. Know how to develop a sense of self, or adult "identity," with consistent behavioral patterns in your intimate relationships, work settings, and social life. If you don't know how to do this, ask a friend you admire who has mastered this ability, or establish a good relationship with a capable psychotherapist.*

~ *Learn how to sustain constancy in love relationships. Foster and sustain intimacy with peer friendships and in love/sexual relationships. If you need help with this, consult a mentor you know who has mastered these qualities, or seek a psychotherapist who specializes in attachment and loss issues.*

~ *Develop a career or work roles congruent with your personality and life goals. Experiment widely with different jobs and tasks and keep evaluating. There are career counselors and consultants available who can provide you with assessments as well as advice for success in your career planning.*

~ *Master basic life skills—acquiring and managing money, managing time, sustaining personal hygiene, and maintaining leisure activities. There are specialists available in each of these areas. The earlier in life you establish sound habits in these basic skills of living, the more you will enjoy the long distance run of adult life.*

None of these is easy or quick, but together they form a platform upon which the rest of your life can be built. If you're a twentysomething, concentrate on these basic building blocks for the future. Don't burn out your engine the first time around the track. Pace yourself into the long haul of life. You've got sixty more years to live your dream! If you follow these general directions you will invent a

I was thinking again of age and of what in each season seems just out of reach, just beyond what is in front of us, a kind of ghost of what we see, to which we offer up our days.
—W. S. Merwin

successful LifeLaunch for your twenties—an experiment with adult life.

THIRTYSOMETHING—
Making-It, 30-38

Most adults spend their thirties "making-it" to become full-fledged citizens of the adult world. This is the time for shaping careers towards successful plateaus, settling down into long-term intimate relationships, having babies, buying things, and eliciting a chorus of approval that you are "making it."

If you're a thirtysomething, you'll probably devote this decade to getting your piece of the rock of adulthood. This is a big decade for acquisitions: a home, furnishings, cars, investments, marriage, children, friends, adult toys, and leisure litanies. The thirties is often the most exhausting decade in the lifecycle, filled with workaholics and time management systems.

This is a major adult period of high expectations and role demands, based largely upon blueprints you obtained from parents, peers, mentors, and society itself. You may be programmed and managed by a "committee in your head," implanted there in your youth. The committee gives a lot of commands, such as "hurry up," "don't do that," "lose weight," and "you should be further along with success than you are."

You probably view this decade as the last time period for reaching your major goals. For many young adults, "40" is a metaphor for "as old as I can ever imagine myself in ascendancy." Your life has a sense of urgency. You are driven by intense internal pressures to arrive at plateaued levels of success, recognition and happiness—as if such plateaus existed!

Thirtysomethings usually find considerable gender diversity which they did not feel in their twenties. This is when men typically over-identify with their jobs and careers, and women find it difficult to balance all the life roles they feel they "should" have, including careers or

People travel to wonder at the height of mountains, and they pass by themselves without wondering.
—St. Augustine

work, home management, mothering, and managing relationships. She is the social chairperson of the entire household, while he drifts deeper into responsibilities and time commitments within his career. This gradual differentiation of roles often takes its toll on dual-career marriages or relationships: her life gets shaped more and more by activities and friends that have little to do with him; his life gets defined by work, work, work.

There are increasingly more men breaking out of this pattern, into a balancing of roles, but the pressures of the workplace are to make work the major measure of success.

Many women who formed careers right out of college are following the male path in their thirties, making marriage and parenthood extremely difficult, or at least, challenging.

How to Maximize Your Thirties—

You can avoid the excesses and pitfalls of the thirties if you develop these abilities:

~ *Increase your personal autonomy by growing more self-confidence and self-esteem. Get psychotherapy if you need it. Stay connected to activities you truly love. Nurture yourself when you're alone. Find peers who are self-confident and learn from them. Join a training group for leadership skills.*

~ *Deepen your primary love relationships. Grow your marriage if you are married. Spend quality time with your children or friends. Practice problem-solving, being assertive, and compromising. Talk about your deep concerns with your closest friends. Be a dependable friend to them.*

~ *Develop your job/career path. Change jobs if you are languishing in the wrong one. Change careers if you see you're headed down the wrong path. Seek ways to use your most prized abilities while getting a necessary funding mechanism for your life. Many thirtysomethings make a powerful career audit in their thirties. Get professional help to do this, to evaluate all your options.*

~ *Create a comprehensive financial plan for managing your money. Seek out a financial planner whom you can pay by the hour for services without having to buy specific forms of investments. You should have an up-to-date will, a diversified portfolio of investments, financial plans for your children's education, and a realistic retirement fund under way.*

~ Deepen your friendships and your leisure life. Find time for people you care about, and for activities that add meaning to your life.

~ Stay in touch with your parents, and be sensitive to their stage in life and their need for your care.

~ Be able to postpone many aspects of personal development. Most of this decade will probably go into "preparation for living" rather than into living itself. Accept the principle of "delayed gratification." Your real deadline is not age forty, but half a century away!

If you follow these general directions you will invent a successful LifeLaunch for your thirties—a beachhead for the rest of your life.

The Midlife Transition, 35-50

The midlife transition (occurring most often between 37 and 45), represents the first heavy adult transition after leaving home as a young adult. This is the likely time for a midlife crisis (meaning a major life transition) if you are going to have one. As Joseph Campbell put it, "Just when you get to the top of your ladder, you realize it is up against the wrong wall."

But don't think of this, or anything else, as a "midlife crisis," because its just one of a number of important turning points in your life. There is no midlife crisis, just one crisis after another for the rest of your life. Almost every transition feels like a crisis. Get used to them. They are normal and they produce wake-up calls that stimulate growth and development. Learn from them. That's what they're there for.

If you're in a midlife transition, you're looking for some fundamental changes in your life:

— from expansiveness and acquisitions towards self-reliance and simplicity;
— from external goals towards internal enrichment,

*Midway life's journey
I was made aware
That I had strayed
into a dark forest,
And the right path
appeared not anymore.
—Dante*

or from relationship maintenance toward external goals;

— from infinite time towards limited time left;

— from parental scripts toward internal ones;

— from body issues toward spiritual themes.

In a midlife transition, turmoil takes many forms:

— *You may be seeking a private life beyond success, beyond being busy, and beyond parenting. If so, concentrate on growing yourself, through reading, writing and quiet solitude.*

— *You may be experiencing a gradual change of consciousness, from organizing the world around your ego needs to organizing your needs around broader themes of meaning and caring. If so, become a volunteer for a cause you believe in, learn to chant, or take a vision quest.*

— *You may be contemplating renewing your marriage, divorcing, making a career change, geographic moves, and other major decisions.*

— *Most often, the midlife transition is a quiet and almost imperceptible change of attitudes and perspective. Enjoy it!*

There is a special quality of life-power available only to those seasoned by struggles of four or more decades. The life-power of this stage can be especially profound.
—Robert Lifton

Almost always, you will reevaluate the attitudes and decisions of your early adult years during the midlife transition, and hunker down for the long haul ahead.

It is just as important to cooperate with the agenda of a transition as it is to launch a successful chapter of your life, so if you are entering the midlife transition, commit yourself to taking stock of your life and becoming regenerated. It's a gift you shouldn't refuse.

FORTYSOMETHING—
Taking Charge, or Individuation, 41-48

This is the decade when you want to be your own person and seek personal autonomy over all the voices in your head. You want to live out of your deep inner resources, reach the profound levels of your maturity, and always be able to retreat from your many roles into the private person within you.

~ If you are entering individuation (becoming a more complete person) you will conduct an audit of your personal commitments, simplify your life, and deepen your key relationships.

~ It is a time for lowering some of your expectations and focusing on what matters most.

~ You will probably seek to shift from quantity to quality issues, from external acquisitions to internal satisfactions, from pleasing others to being your own person.

~ During this period, you are likely to experience increases in self-responsible behavior, an entrepreneurial interest, and a movement toward spirituality. Many fortysomethings report a profound spiritual stirring in their lives, helping them move beyond their ego needs to the broader issues and wonder around them.

~ During individuation you discover more of your "human imprint" (the validity of all six adult passions or values, and an acceptance of the renewal cycle as a positive process). Some of the themes are body changes, changes in values, changes in rewards sought at work, caring for aging parents, caring for children, and the realization that time is running out.

~ Your growth impetus is toward becoming accountable to yourself, anchored in integrity and personal depth, driven from within and not by external forces.

~ But individuation often has its price. Alliances with careers, mates, children, and friends made during the twenties and thirties often get bruised, trashed, abandoned, or transformed by fortysomethings. This does not have to happen. You can learn to be YOU without alienating yourself from family, friends, and commitments.

I am now forty-five, and I believe that I am more vital and alive now than at any other time of my life. My transitions were more useful to my journey than I had wanted to believe while I was in the midst of them.
—Marvin Banasky

How to Maximize Your Forties—

~ *Know how to rearrange your busy life around your own essence and core values. Eliminate activities that don't add meaning to your life.*

~ *Become your own best friend. Maintain a positive inner dialogue, with humor and perspective. Take care of yourself.*

~ Nurture and develop your spiritual resources for future development. Consciously define your spiritual life and how it relates to solitude, nature, reading, travel, service and organized groups.

~ See your life as "time left" rather than "time lived." Feel grateful for each day and invest in human capital rather than things. If you follow these general directions you will invent a successful LifeLaunch for your forties—as you take charge of your life.

Transition into Fiftysomething—48-53

So much has been written about the age 40 transition that few people know much about the transition from 40 to 50, which for many is extremely profound. This transition takes you away from the fortysomething autonomy/take-charge themes in the direction of becoming more outgoing, lighthearted, and diffuse. You leave the Hamlet-like personal heaviness of the forties behind so you can grow a lifestyle with more sharing, optimism, caring, and fun.

FIFTYSOMETHING— Emergence of Interdependence, 51-59

Women who have spent their thirties and forties raising children as well as sustaining careers may use much of their fifties completing the tasks of individuation begun in their forties. They may reenter educational programs, travel alone, take up hobbies, or begin new friendships. Assertiveness and self-directed behaviors increase, along with the caring connections that most women sustain as part of their core reality.

Men and women who invested in individuation during their forties move in this decade into a broad celebration of life. The emphasis is upon living, not getting ready to live; upon realized expectations, not grandiose future ones. Friendships typically increase, as do humor and leisure interests. The focus is upon interdependence — sharing, working things out, and enjoying the journey.

How to Maximize Your Fifties—

~ *Develop more inner-driven behaviors:*
  — *An ease to enjoy many things;*
  — *A focus on the here-and-now rather than yesterday or tomorrow, comfort with directness, compromise, and managing conflict;*
  — *An inner contentment with life.*

~ *Broaden and deepen your expressions of intimacy or caring—to be close and affectionate with more people. Friendships will increase in importance, mostly with same-gender people, but with cross-gender people as well.*

~ *Develop an ability to change your leadership style from active mastery to passive mastery—exerting influence through policies, supervisory roles, episodic events, and symbolic actions instead of daily, hands-on roles.*

~ *Find proper outlets for your increased social caring, often leading to new leadership roles in the post-parental years.*

~ *Tap deeper dimensions of personal meaning from travel and leisure, and begin to see play as important a feature in your life as work has been.*

~ *Know how to create a simpler and more fulfilling time schedule.*

~ *Know how to enrich your spiritual sensitivity to the world around you.*

~ *Enjoy living a day at a time.*

This is the decade that many researchers report receives the highest ratings of any adult decade for "life satisfaction" and "marital satisfaction." Fiftysomethings often report high self-esteem, comfort with life, and commitment to the art of living. If you're approaching your fifties, why don't you interview three people in their late 50s and ask them how this decade has been for them. *You will probably find that the 50s* **LifeLaunch** *is one that you will enjoy profoundly.*

1996: Paul McCartney turned 54 this year; so did Aretha Franklin. Bob Dylan is 55, as are Frank Zappa, Paul Simon and Art Garfunckel. Raquel Welch is 55, Robert Redford is 59. The broad concept of middle age is starting later and lasting longer—and looking better than ever before. Contrary to conventional wisdom, many people find that the 50s is actually a period of reduced stress and anxiety.
—Melinda Beck

Transition into Sixtysomething—58-63

Under the banner of "retirement," this shifting of gears has enormous social approval and resources to draw upon. This transition often involves major changes: geographic relocation, marital renewal or change of partners, economic downsizing, and departure from social contexts which provided you with meaning and validation while beginning new contexts of adventure and challenge.

SIXTYSOMETHING— Beginning Again, 61-68

Retirement no longer means to disengage from work or life, but to begin again, with all the old options (work, intimacy, family, leisure, travel, leadership roles), plus an increased drive toward living life to its fullest on a day-by-day basis. We call it "protirement," meaning to place yourself ahead into the activities and life style of your choice-to continue to pursue the "best years of your life".

Most sixtysomethings spend this decade living their beliefs and seeking quality experiences. Assuming that finances and health are positive assets, the sixties often provide one of the best decades of the adult years, when you can do what you want to do and become who you want to be.

In the twenty-first century, few sixtysomethings sit around feeling old and impaired, waiting for a bell to announce their demise. Rather, they seek vintage living and quality choices. Being sixty is just another time to begin again—with more life experience, money, and social resources for both enjoying the experience and deepening the journey ahead.

How to Maximize Your Sixties—

~ The single most important ability is a capacity to vision and dream again, to imagine ways to add value to your life as old overtakes young.

~ Learn how to reduce external necessities to a minimum. Sixtysomethings launch a quest for simplicity, demonstrated by a reduction of things, possessions, and routine roles.

This year I turned 60. I have a sense of urgency about accomplishing my work—a sense of limited time—but there is no frenzy in it, no hanging cloud raining dark thoughts of approaching infirmities or death.
—Larry L. King

~ *Deepen intimacy through friendships, hobbies, travel, and work. Bonds with others are just as important in your sixties and seventies as earlier in life.*

~ *Renew your marriage or intimate relationships. Talk, touch, and learn new ways to care for each other.*

~ *Deepen your personal spirituality or presence in the world, with intense living and celebrating in the here and now.*

~ *Commit to the dictate, "If you don't use it, you lose it," referring to every organ of your body, and every vital connection with the world around you. Think, read, talk, travel, contribute, pray, bless, rejoice, and learn, learn, learn. Refuse to disengage from any part of life that keeps adding meaning to your future.*

~ *You will probably experience a desire to mentor—sharing your acquired competence as a professional and as a human being with others—particularly your progeny and younger persons in your specialized field. Mentoring becomes a basic form of personal and social caring, personal leadership roles that can influence the future.*

If you follow these general directions you will invent a successful LifeLaunch for your sixties, a launch with more freedom to follow your own vision and values than ever before in your life.

Transition into Seventysomething—
68-71

By now transitions are quite familiar, but in this one there are issues which make moving ahead into another decade difficult: body problems, from aches and pains to disease and accidents; compounded losses: of friends, fewer opportunities for work and service, social and economic convulsions.

This transition is the gateway to a productive or unproductive elderhood, so it is of great significance to your journey ahead. The secret is to remain an on-purpose person—with a proactive agenda that is heavier on celebration and contribution than on doing and neediness.

To be young is to be fresh, lively, eager, quick to learn; to be mature is to be done, complete, sedate, tired. What if we consider a different perspective? To be young is to be unripe, unfinished, raw, awkward, unskilled, inept; to be mature is to be ready, whole, adept, wise. How valid are our glorification of youth and our shame about having lived many years?
—Lillian E. Troll

SEVENTYSOMETHING
AND EIGHTYSOMETHING—
Living the Fullness, Summing Up the Story, 71-89

Seventysomethings and eightysomethings are the elders of our society. Although the lifecycle is being extended into the eighties and nineties as we learn to eat and exercise more wisely, people in these two decades see their ranks thin out dramatically, through accidents, illness, and death.

We write these words to those who are eager to live as fully as possible in these decades. Sometimes seventysomethings and eightysomethings are recognized and consulted for their wisdom, integrity, and cultural perspective. They often inspire others with their optimism and hope. They model the fullness of life. They are Menschen, mentors, guides to the future. They are the consummate cultural resources, consultants, and symbols. Their blessings are the force that links generation after generation.

Think not of yourselves, O Chiefs, nor of your own generation. Think of continuing generations of our families, think of our grandchildren and of those yet unborn, whose faces are coming from beneath the ground.
—Iroquois Chief

They are the most profound bearers of culture, consciousness, and spirit—the cultural CD Roms walking among us. If they remain vital, they have perspective, because they link the past with the present and future. There can be no greater time in adult life than this, however unheralded and underutilized it is by our society. If seventysomethings and eightysomethings don't speak and act, and if we don't listen and learn, history itself is injured and deprived.

There is no cultural script for finding meaning and fulfillment in our seventies and eighties. We, ourselves have to write these scripts, both individually and collectively. By 2020, we will have created a social sense of purpose for elders over seventy.

How to Maximize
Your Seventies and Eighties

~ *Initiate and maintain any "work" or "career" interest you have.*

~ *Keep rearranging your priorities and taking advantage of opportunities to connect to the world around you.*

~ *Sustain leadership roles in your community and develop a caring candor you never before had. You can "get away" with truth-telling now.*

~ *Spend time meditating, introspecting, and "summing up" your life. Keep a clear slate.*

~ *Refuse to look in on your past life as if your present life and future were less important. Refuse to depress yourself by looking backwards. Resist constant reminiscing.*

~ *Live your hopes and expectations, on a daily basis. Reach out, touch, greet.*

~ *Remind yourself often that your own life is worthy, purposive, and important, and that there is always something of value you can be thinking or doing every day.*

~ *Transcend ordinary problems with humor, perspective, and trust.*

~ *Be grateful and appreciative.*

~ *Endorse, sponsor, and bless others, particularly younger people.*

~ *Sustain healthy social networks for support and expression.*

~ *Get advice and help as you need it, for sustaining adequate levels of health, nutrition, leisure, and projects.*

~ *If you are approaching your seventies, write a letter to yourself at age 79, giving instructions on how to live. Read your letter often.*

~ *If you are approaching your eighties, read biographies of resilient and successful eighty to ninety-year-olds.*

~ *If you are approaching your nineties, follow this same list. Look ahead!*

I am 78 years old and I believe the elderly would and should serve as mentors and guides to oncoming generations. We should guide young people to think always about how to improve life in this country, both political and private.
—Sarah McClendon

If seventysomethings and eightysomethings can elude the poison of ageism—in their heads as well as in their social experience—they represent the largest untapped human resource in our society. Take this LifeLaunch with the spirit of the pioneers who forged their way through our geographical wildernesses years ago. This is a new frontier for human potential and creativity, to articulate enduring values, to insist on planetary wholeness, and to call us all away from our busy lives into the business of living fully in these days. Society can not afford to keep you in its margins, and you deserve the mainstream for your own fulfillment. Let it be!

DYING—
The Final Transition

Dying is the final stage of living. The way you face dying is shaped by the way you have managed "letting go" in many transitions throughout your life. If you have learned to trust the unknown, to find peace in resignation, and to search for new paths in darkness, then this adventure will have some familiarity.

People who know they are dying often rise to levels of clarity and boldness about their lives which they never before experienced. The experience of dying elicits honest, blunt words of personal truth. It stretches the imagination to picture yourself in relation to non-being, and to picture the world without you, and you without the world. Those are awesome and terrifying mysteries of dying.

Those who find dying meaningless and negative probably found old age meaningless and negative, and maybe the adult years as well. If you are always pursuing the cutting edge of your personal journey, dying can be a refinement of your spirituality, and a discovery of completeness and peace, not a denial of your life.

And the Dance Goes On

We are not obliged to know everything about the adult lifecycle, only what we need to know to renew and direct the years we are in. Find a depth of comfort with life as you have it, along with a fierce determination to make improvements in the direction of your beliefs.

~ *You have an inner child. Honor, welcome, and cherish the child within you.*

~ *You have a young adult experience. Accept it, warts and all, with its innocence, yearnings, and presumptions.*

~ Some of you have a midlife experience—holding the world on your backs, day and night, expecting life to go on forever.

~ Some of you are elders, committed to the art of living, a day at a time, as you are marginalized by society and your understandable loneliness.

Truth is, we all need one another, and at every age we have more in common than we have differences. We are all the time knitting ourselves together, and pulling ourselves apart, in the great cycle of renewal—which is the dance of life. In the past fifty years there has been a definite trend toward separating age groups into demographic markets and geographic isolation. What we need most at this turn in history is inclusion, cooperation, and support—one for all and all for one, throughout the whole earth.

CHAPTER 8

MAP 5
The Adult Learning Agenda

Becoming the Best that
You Can Be

This final map—Map 5—completes your preparation for creating a new LifeLaunch.

~ In Map 1 you gained mastery over your experience of change, so that you can find increased comfort and effectiveness within the turbulence of today.

~ Map 2 led you to choose your emerging priorities for the next chapter of your life. You identified your core values and your compelling sense of purpose.

~ Map 3 helped you reappraise your social activities and roles—the strategic assignments in which you can best find fulfillment at this time in your life. Relating your key roles to your current, core values is essential to a healthy LifeLaunch.

~ Map 4 added a positive perspective on how to proceed through all your years with sufficient information and humor for getting older creatively. Stay "on course" with your life so you can pursue your best options no matter what your age.

~ **Map 5 is a cornucopia of adult learning items, from which you pick and choose those special items that will illuminate your path and improve your skills for your next LifeLaunch. Your best future is discovered and invented through learning.**

MAP 5

THE ADULT LEARNING AGENDA

__ 1. What do I need to unlearn?

__ 2. What new information do I need?

__ 3. How do I increase my personal competence?

__ 4. What new technical skills do I need?

__ 5. How can I stay anchored in my values?

__ 6. Where are my best learning environments?

__ 7. Who are my real teachers and mentors?

Adults who are truly alive are always learning. Learning, for them, is an attitude, a habit, a way of life. To learn is to turn problems into investigations, and crises into opportunities. When you are learning you discover new ways to approach some unknown, and you desensitize your fear of other unknowns in your life.

Learning is self-initiated change, when you try to replace some dark spot in your mind with clear concepts. Learning helps you gain increased comfort with newness everywhere in your life. When you are engaged in the art of learning, the changing world around you bothers you much less. In an age of unbelievable turbulence, learning is the most important human modality for empowering adult life.

Few of us use learning to our full advantage. It is all too easy to lock ourselves into what we've already learned as the world spins on into new paradigms and technologies. Many of us replace our youthful habits for learning with midlife habits for unwinding on evenings and weekends, leaving new learning to others. You have a choice: rest on your oars and let your boat drift along or keep learning new nautical skills, so you can proceed to preferred destinations.

Adult learning is about discovering, not memorizing. It's about awakening, not passing tests. It's visceral discovery, not mental schooling. Adult learning is most frequently related to experiential concerns, not to formal instruction or teaching. It is self-directed inquiry, reflection, and application.

The chief object of education is not to learn things but to unlearn things.
—G. K. Chesterton

Real learning unleashes joy and excitement, confidence and determination, in addition to acquiring new skills and competencies. Learning links you to future possibilities and paths for moving ahead.

Learning also addresses the fear of aging. Adults at any age who fail to keep up with the acceleration of learning take on stereotypical "old" behaviors—passivity, fear, and lowered self-esteem. Continuous learning keeps you vital, awake, and expectant.

The Seven Adult Learning Questions

Before you launched your first adult life structure, you went to school for years to get ready for the great adventure ahead—your grown-up years. You earned degrees, got work experience, learned how to manage yourself in many settings, became an expert in something, and settled down for the long haul.

Education is not filling a bucket but lighting a fire.
—William Butler Yeats

Your training for that first adult life structure took over twenty years, and when you launched your dream, you may have lacked experience but you didn't lack careful preparation and powerful determination.

During the rest of your life you will have lots of experience, but probably never have such intense learning preparation, unless you make it happen. Society wound you up for the first launching, but you have to wind yourself up for every new LifeLaunch. There are at least *seven questions to ask yourself* to define the new learning you need before designing your plan for the next chapter of your life:

1. UNLEARNING. What do I have to *unlearn* if I'm going to master the future I truly want? What patterns of thinking that served me well earlier in my life are now *in the way* of what I really want to do and become?

How do you discover what you need to unlearn?

~ Ask yourself, "What am I resisting the most? What can I do to become proactive in that part of my life?"

~ Ask your friends what they think you need to unlearn.

~ Ask your boss what you need to unlearn.

~ Ask your spouse or intimate other what you need to unlearn.

~ Spend your time at a convention or trade show where the cutting edge of your knowledge base is thoroughly exposed, and ask yourself the question, "What do I need to unlearn, in order to break out of my set patterns so I can learn how to become, and not merely to hold on?"

2. NEW INFORMATION AND KNOWLEDGE.
What *new information and knowledge* do I need in order to be at my best *at this time in my life*? What information and knowledge can I legitimately *avoid* in order to prevent information overload?

In our kind of world you have to keep up in the areas of your special concerns, and to do that you have to filter out media, infobases, and the clamor of the world that have little to do with the path you are on. The secret to acquiring new information and knowledge is to know how to focus on those areas in which you want continuous information and cutting-edge expertise.

The flip side is saying no to the endless intrusions upon your learning time, particularly by phone, television, and other media sources. If they don't inform the path you're on, or add meaning to your life, just say no.

~ **Read, read, read.** In our technical age, reading remains the number one highway into the further reaches of your mind. Make your reading schedule the steady core of your learning agenda: newspapers, magazines, books of all sorts, professional journals, and computer-based materials. If at all possible, join reading groups so you can discuss new ideas with others.

~ **On-line network groups,** like Internet. Women's Wire, Compuserve, and many others can dazzle you with what's going on in your own field, and stimulate you to get learning.

~ **Intensive seminars and workshops.** Not the one-day entertainment varieties, but the three to five day group learning formats that engage you profoundly in basic learning.

~ **Episodic learning**. Travel alone, climb a mountain, take an adventure, conduct a vision quest, or join an adult education class in some new and intriguing subject. Spend some time working and living in a third world country if you possibly can, to discover how people very different from you live and work. Jolt your routines to discover ones that connect you better to the future.

The only person who is educated is the one who has learned how to learn…and change.
—Carl Rogers

~ **Advanced certification and degree programs.** Advanced learning programs for midlife and older adults exist throughout the land, providing thousands of adults every year a rite of passage from one LifeLaunch to another. Some of them involve only evenings or occasional weekends. Some use distance learning techniques such as computers, telephone meetings, and regional conferences so that students can remain at home and at work while engaged in serious study. These programs often provide not only intensive learning opportunities, but the discovery of friends, networking contacts, and personal/professional renewal.

3. PERSONAL COMPETENCE. What *life skills* do I want and need to develop, to be alive and purposive in all that I do?

Life skills refer to your general human abilities to sustain relationships, be an effective parent, manage conflict, travel, and feel at home in the world. Life skills are abilities like listening, speaking, writing, negotiating, and meditating. Today's world has many technocrats and executives who have outstanding behaviors in their specialized fields, but who haven't learned the basic human skills for managing the microsystems of their own lives. It's never too late to learn life skills, and to claim your personal competence.

Maybe I'll play well today. Maybe I'll win. Maybe I won't play well and won't win. But whatever happens, I'll learn something from it.
—Jack Nicklaus

~ **Psychotherapy** often performs the function of teaching personal life skills, and helps adults get anchored within their own true abilities and values.

~ **Churches, adult education, and other community organizations** have learning programs, trips, and training for learning basic life skills.

~ **Some adults discover these skills through short-term commitments in volunteer service roles** in the community, or working with the Peace Corps or any of the many worldwide service organizations.

4. TECHNICAL SKILLS. What *technical skills* do I need to improve at this time in my life—perhaps specialized skills in accounting, management, or other professional abilities—for increasing my practitioning proficiencies at this time in my life?

~ **Ask your boss and work friends** for ways to pursue professional skills in your career field.

~ **Take advantage of the ongoing training** and credentialing programs of the professional organizations in your specialized area.

~ **Join a network group** working on critical issues in your field.

~ **Create weekly or monthly meetings** of "experts" like yourself from various companies in your geographic area, to provide each other with updates and learning challenges.

Try to know everything of something and something of everything.
—Lord Brougham

5. VALUES AND LEADERSHIP ROLES. What do I need to learn to keep my life *aligned to my values and leadership roles?*

Sooner or later, you become a leader—of yourself, and perhaps much more. You engage your values through acts of inspiration, persuasion, and example. Leadership does not have to be full-time or all consuming; it needs to be fulfilling and meaningful. True leadership grows out of your own integrity and concerns, not polls or desired rewards. Most midlife and elder adults want to become a positive influence within the culture around them— through children and grandchildren, organizations they believe in, and the political process itself.

Leadership begins when you lead your own human agenda in a purposive way. Leadership is anchored in your deep, dependable qualities, not in memorized affirmations or roles. Start with personal leadership, and you will soon find all kinds of ways to exert influence beyond yourself—*apprentice, intern, volunteer, join a leadership training course.*

*Tell me, I'll forget.
Show me,
I may remember.
But involve me and
I'll understand.*
—Chinese Proverb

6. LEARNING ENVIRONMENTS. Where are *the learning environments* and resources that I need at this time in my life?

Since the whole global village is your campus, scope out your best learning centers and formats—seminars, mentors, conferences, books, study groups, certification programs, advanced degrees, travel, and get yourself connected.

Don't think of learning as something you have to purchase from some teacher or educational service. Learning is what you need to acquire because you are ready. There is a Chinese saying that when the pupil is ready, the teacher will appear. The same is true for learning environments: When you're ready to learn, the learning opportunities will appear.

Be responsible for identifying the best format for the kind of learning you are seeking. There is no paucity of adult learning opportunities near and far. Seek out the ones that serve your needs, and commit to the learning you want.

7. TEACHERS AND MENTORS. Who are *my teachers and mentors*, at this time in my life?

Adults do not want to sit at the feet of mere knowledge experts; they want to learn from masters—persons who have applied knowledge to themselves and their professions, people who have unconscious competence integrated into their behavior.

That is why so many conventional college professors do not appeal to midlife adults as appropriate teachers. They are often experts in a cognitive field, not masters of how that field connects to life around them. Adult students want to apply knowledge and to gain mastery beyond knowledge.

The new adult teacher is a mentor, Mensch, or master—someone who lives and breathes "viscerally" what the learner wants to learn. There are such experts available around the world today. You have to find them and hire them, and create your own "learning system." You

Trouble in adulthood often can be defined as people being in situations without the knowledge, skills, and other tools needed to cope with those situations. Adults need to understand that they can learn their way out of commonplace kinds of trouble—whether it occurs as loss of job, loss of spouse, or loss of health. Learning provides a route to a new career, a different kind of family life, or renewed health.
—Americans in Transition

may not find them at conventional learning institutions, although they are there, too.

Your Turn!

In your journal or notebook, identify your learning objectives for the next chapter of your life.

1. Information and Knowledge
Learning   Training Program   Dates for
Objective   or Trainer   Training
(List those you need and want)

2. Personal Competence and Life Skills
Learning   Training Program   Dates for
Objective   or Trainer   Training
(List those you need and want)

3. Technical Skills
Learning   Training Program   Dates for
Objective   or Trainer   Training
(List those you need and want)

4. Values and Leadership
Learning   Training Program   Dates for
Objective   or Trainer   Training
(List those you need and want)

5. In your time management system, write in all your learning commitments for the next year, so you treat learning as being as important as all the other things you spend time doing. If you make learning your primary personal commitment, you will find the future a creative and promising place. You will also find yourself more awake and eager to move ahead into your next LifeLaunch.

Self-education is, I firmly believe, the only kind of education there is.
—Isaac Asimov

To be awake is to be alive. We must learn to reawaken and keep ourselves awake, not by mechanical aids, but by an infinite expectation of the dawn.
—Henry David Thoreau

Section III

Launch the Next Chapter of Your Life

CHAPTER 9

Get a Plan
Walk Your Talk

THE LIFELAUNCH FORMULA

STEP 1

FEEL YOUR SENSE OF PURPOSE

The Awe, Mystery, and Ecstasy of the Not-Yet

Tap Your Spiritual Energy

"I am alive and expectant"

Purpose is your WHY.

STEP 2

IMAGINE THE FUTURE YOU PREFER

Vision, Dream, Picture, Wonder

Identify Your Core Values, Your Deep Passions

"I am drawn irresistibly in this direction"

Vision is your WHAT.

STEP 3

FIND WORDS AND REALITY PATHS TO GUIDE YOU

Put Your Expectations and Goals in the Form of a Story

Identify Your Preferred Roles, Relationships, Networks

Find a Funding Mechanism

Make a Plan to Get from Here to There

Create Action Steps and Time Lines

Commit to Your Personal Mission

"I/We will do and become it"

Plans are your HOW.

This chapter guides you through the steps to follow as you put together the details of your next LifeLaunch. First, give some thought to how you might sabotage your plan or be sabotaged by unanticipated outside forces.

Take a Look at What Might Go Wrong

It's one thing to get a good fix on how you want your next chapter in life to be, and quite another to make it happen. As you nudge your way closer to planning and launching, take a hard look at the dark sides of yourself and the world around you.

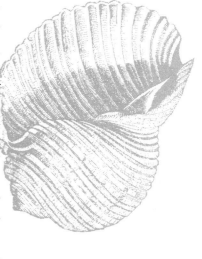

~ "There's always something," Gilda Radner used to say, and there is always some reason why our lives don't proceed as planned. "Life is difficult," Scott Peck asserts, and he's right. We calculate our wants much better than the dark undercurrent running against us—even within us.

~ The world is hazardous. We are very skilled at expecting a perfect world, and then being undone when something goes wrong. What might get in the way of your LifeLaunch and how can prepare for those possibilities?

~ Sometimes we are hazards to our own world. We are very capable of subverting ourselves and others even when things are going well. How might you undermine your own plan?

While we can't eliminate all the boulders on our path, we can learn how to live with them more creatively, and sometimes gain an upper hand.

~ First of all, put the boulders on your path into two groups: external threats and internal obstacles .

~ Second, examine the external threats and internal obstacles that might subvert your upcoming LifeLaunch, to see how you might get around them .

~ Third, build specific strategies into your plan for managing your external threats and internal obstacles.

You will hereafter be called to account for depriving yourself of the good things which the world lawfully allows.
—Talmud

External Threats

An external threat is something that comes at you from the world around you. These are the non-psychological, reality problems and issues that we can't avoid in our global village today. Some possible external threats for the last half-decade of the twentieth century include the following. **Rate each one on a scale of 1-3 with 1 being extremely likely, 2 being somewhat likely, and 3 being extremely unlikely.**

Man is what he believes.
—Anton Chekhov

*What a strange
machine man is!
You fill him with bread,
wine, fish and radishes,
and out of him
come sighs, laughter
and dreams.*
—Nikos Kazantzakis

External Threats	Your Ratings		
	1	2	3
~ Violence			
~ Inflation			
~ TV			
~ Sexism			
~ Aging parents			
~ Wars			
~ Inflation			
~ Diseases			
~ Car Accident			
~ Tornado			
~ Hurricane			
~ Drought			
~ Addictions			
~ Ageism			
~ AIDS			
~ Being fired			
~ Divorce			
~ Pollution			
~ Guns			
~ $$$$$			
~ Poverty			
~ Racism			
~ Physical abuse			
~ Recession			
~ Loss of jobs			
~ Overpopulation			
~ Earthquake			
~ Collapse of a social system			
~ Dysfunctional family			
~ Death of a hero			

Internal Obstacles

An internal obstacle is something you do to make it difficult to reach your goals and to feel good. These are internal habits that keep you from being at your best, and from being comfortable and committed to winning at life. Some possible internal obstacles you might want to consider include the following. Rate each one on a scale of 1-3 with 1 being extremely likely, 2 being somewhat likely, and 3 being extremely unlikely:

Internal Obstacles	Your Ratings		
	1	2	3
~ Old habits			
~ Failure			
~ Success			
~ Denial			
~ Sloth			
~ Ageism			
~ Depression			
~ Alcoholism			
~ Hopelessness			
~ Anger			
~ Blaming			
~ Helplessness			
~ Low self-esteem			
~ Stress			
~ Self deprecation			
~ Fear			
~ Lying			
~ Lack of time management			
~ Resistance to change			
~ Feeling betrayed			
~ Feeling abandoned			
~ Too much or too little $$			
~ Unreasonable expectations			
~ Procrastination			
~ Perfectionism			
~ Loneliness			

How can you learn not to place these on your own path, particularly the ones you rated 1 or 2? Once you identify real external threats and internal obstacles that you are likely to face in the next chapter of your life, ask yourself the following questions, and come up with initial answers you can count on, *before* you write your plan. Write out your responses in your journal or workbook:

What are Your External Threats?

1. What are your major worries about the world around you right now? How do they affect you and reduce your effectiveness? How can you change the way you let these matters reduce your effectiveness?

2. To what extent are your "external threats" actually media creations that aren't in reality as bad as they seem?

3. Which ones are, in fact, threatening your future and need to be addressed in some way so you can believe in your future? How will you address your most pressing reality issues that are working against your journey ahead?

What are Your Internal Obstacles?

1. How have you messed up your plans or got in your own way in years past? How does your personal pattern of subversion work? If you really don't know, ask someone who knows you really well to give you feedback on this.

2. Knowing you can't totally eliminate these thoughts, beliefs, and habits, how can you minimize their negative impact on your next chapter?

Who are the persons you can count on to help you think things through if internal obstacles and/or external threats get in the way of your plan? Identify your critical support group now. For financial affairs? Legal guidance? Relationship issues? Career advice and redirection? Personal confusion? Exerting political influence?

Summarize Your Findings
from the Five Maps in This Book

Before writing a plan for the next chapter of your life, make a summary in your journal or notebook of what you gleaned from the five maps, using the outline below as a guideline. If you already have these findings clearly in mind, move right ahead with this chapter.

MAP 1
Composing Life Chapters and Transitions—
The Renewal Cycle

1. Are you currently in a life chapter or in a transition (see pages 47-63)?

2. Which of the four steps are you in (see pages 49-63)?

_____ **Phase One —** *Launching*, challenged by a new beginning, clear goals, and available resources.

_____ **Phase Two —** *Stuck in the Doldrums,* sensing decline, resisting change, feeling disenchanted.

_____ **Minitransition—** *Improving the Chapter You're In*

_____ **Phase Three —** *Cocooning*, taking time out to heal, renew yourself, and tap your core values.

_____ **Phase Four —** *Exploring the World Again*, through learning, experimenting, networking, training, and getting ready for Phase One again.

MAP 2
Leading a Deliberate Life—
Living with Passion and Purpose

3. List, in order of importance, from one (the highest) to six (the lowest) your core values *for the next chapter of your life* (see pages 65-71):

___ Personal Power

___ Achievement

___ Intimacy

___ Play and Creativity

___ Search for Meaning

___ Compassion and Contribution

4. Indicate some of the **results or passionate destinations** you want, during the next chapter of your life, from the top three core values just indicated (numbers 1, 2, and 3 on pages 71-72).

He who has a why can endure any how.
—Nietzsche

5. On page 73 you translated your core values into a "purpose statement" for the next chapter of your life. Review what you wrote in your journal or notebook, and either endorse it and use it—if what you wrote remains valid and compelling—or write a more up-to-date version that expresses your sense of purpose at this time (see page 130).

MAP 3
Life's Assignments—
Balancing the Parts of Your Life

6. Indicate those activities and roles that are most important for the next chapter of your life (see pages 75-86):
_____ Personal (list specific activities and roles in this category that are important for your next chapter)
_____ Couple (list specific activities and roles in this category that are important for your next chapter)
_____ Family (list specific activities and roles in this category that are important for your next chapter)
_____ Work (list specific activities and roles in this category that are important for your next chapter)
_____ Social Connections (list specific activities and roles in this category that are important for your next chapter)

7. How do you want to change your activities and roles in your next chapter? (see page 84).

MAP 4
The Grand Adventure
Across the Life Cycle

8. What are your central developmental tasks for becoming your best self at this time in your life—your current challenges for deepening your life? Look up your likely decade agenda—and the ones before and after. Then formulate your major areas for growth. What are your emergent forces, concerns, values, and spiritual direction for the next chapter of your life? (pages 87-106)

MAP 5
The Adult Learning Agenda
Becoming the Best You Can Be

9. What are your responses to the Seven Adult Learning Questions (pages 107-115)?
— What do I need to unlearn?
— What new information do I need?
— What are the areas I need to increase my personal competence?
— What technical skills do I need?
— What are my core values and how do I translate them into leadership roles?
— What are my best learning environments?
— Who are my real teachers and mentors?

10. What are your strategic learning objectives for the next chapter of your life? (page 115)

11. Summarize your learning agenda.

When you are inspired by some great purpose, some extraordinary project, all your thoughts break their bounds: Your mind transcends limitations, your consciousness expands in every direction and you find yourself in a new, great and wonderful world. Dormant forces, faculties and talents become alive, and you discover yourself to be a greater person by far than you ever dreamed yourself to be.
—Patanjali

Examine the summary you've just made, and your entire journal or workbook, to see if there are goals or action steps that should go into your plan. Now:

Put each goal or action step on a Post-It and stick it on the table or wall where you're going to do your planning. This way you can see all the planning possibilities you've already identified as you move into full-time planning.

How Will the Next Chapter of Your Life Turn Out?

Freedom consists not in refusing to recognize anything above us, but in respecting something which is above us; for by respecting it, we raise ourselves to it, and by our very acknowledgment, prove that we bear within ourselves what is higher, and are worthy to be on a level with it.
—Goethe

1. If you were granted one wish for the next chapter of your life, what would it be?

2. If you could live out the next chapter of your life in any place in the world, where would you go?

3. If you could hire three advisors to guide the next chapter of your life, who would they be?

4. If you could inherit money to fund the next chapter of your life, how much would that be?

5. If you could move now to some future point in your life, what are you doing and who is with you?

6. If you have children, how would you like them to be five years from now?

7. If you were recognized as a gigantic success at the end of the next chapter of your life, what would you be known for?

There is no tougher challenge that we face than to accept personal responsibility for not only what we are but also what we can be.
—David McNally

8. If you could have friends attribute one quality to you at the end of the next chapter of your life, what would you want it to be?

9. If you could have someone from the past work for you as your personal assistant in the next chapter of your life, who would it be and why?

10. If you could provide a title for the next chapter of your life, what would it be?

The rest of this chapter is devoted to a proven, detailed process for creating a successful LifeLaunch. Follow it systematically in three steps:

~ **Identify your purpose**
~ **Write out your vision of the future you prefer**
~ **Write out your plan for the next chapter of your life**

Step 1. *What Is Your Purpose at this Time in Your Life?*

Purpose, Vision, and Plans are like three doors leading to a LifeLaunch. The first of these is "purpose," your raison d'etre, your answer to "Why am I here?"

No one has much of a life without hope and belief in the future.

Purpose is a profound commitment to a compelling expectation for this time in your life. No one has the same sense of purpose throughout an entire life. You get a different formulation of your purpose at different ages and places.

~ Purpose is not the same as goals. It is a greater force than goals, and less precise.
~ Purpose is an expression of your ultimate concerns.
~ Purpose is the sum of your yearnings for what you may become, or devote your life to becoming.
~ Purpose comes from your basic belief system, whatever it is.
~ Purpose inspires the activities of your life.
~ Purpose provides meaning for your life.
~ Purpose generates commitment beyond your daily needs to the most lofty reaches of your mind and soul.

You feel your sense of purpose deep within you, in what Carl Jung called your inner "self," that part of you that transcends your ego needs and connects you to lasting values and meaning. Purpose, which is anchored in "being," provides meaning to "doing," "loving," and "playing." Some people find purpose through their faith, often

The entrepreneur is essentially a visualizer and an actualizer. He can visualize something, and when he visualizes it he sees exactly how to make it happen.
—Robert Schwartz

their belief in God. But people who live without a religious belief system need purpose just as much as religious believers. Our lives don't function well or long without purpose. Purpose used to be abundant in American lives. It is now scarce, and we all suffer when any of us lacks it.

After reviewing what you said about your purpose in life, in Map 2 on page 73, update your statement of purpose for the next chapter of your life. Write it out in your journal or workbook. Keep it simple, short, and compelling. Rewrite it until it feels like a magnet pulling you ahead. Talk it over with your closest friends, because while purpose is highly personal, it is also social and spiritual.

Step 2. What Is Your Vision or Dream for the Next Chapter of Your Life?

Your purpose distills into a vision or dream, which is more precise and clear than your purpose, but less precise and clear than your plan. You almost always begin a life chapter with a dream. "We hold these truths to be self-evident," said a founding father of our country, as he laid out the American dream that has been a major social force guiding our country for over 200 years. "I have a dream," yearned Martin Luther King in Washington, D.C., as he painted a picture of equality and fairness in America, and made it his full time agenda.

The dream comes first. Reality chases after the dream, to make it happen.

~ A vision or dream declares what is important, purposive, and valuable for your life ahead.

~ It is a poetic picture, not a literal statement.

~ A vision/dream is visceral yearning, not a wish list. You don't dream for a new car, an exotic vacation, or even a new career. Rather, you envision—in your mind's eye—an overall picture for your future life—working, living, contributing, and having fun.

~ A vision is a spiritual promise of a new quality of life, a deeper sense of being, a value-added life. It's a promise

Are you in earnest? Then seize this very minute. What you can do, or dream you can, begin it; boldness has genius, power and magic in it; only engage and then the mind grows heated; begin, and then the work will be completed.
—Goethe

I expect to spend the rest of my life in the future so I want to be reasonably sure what kind of future it's going to be. That is my reason for planning.
—C. F. Kettering

that is convincing. To think it is to go for it. It feels right, and it's going to happen, because it's already happening. It feels that simple and sure.

~ A real vision feels like it is pulling you toward it from without and pushing you towards it from within. Like a sail it guides you toward shores you need to reach; like a rudder it guides you—a day at a time—with dependable direction.

~ A dream is a haunting refrain. You know you have a vision when it won't let you go, and others are attracted to it in you.

~ A dream inspires and motivates; it doesn't order you around. As far as we know, human beings are the only creatures on earth capable of envisioning a future and then setting about to make it happen.

~ A dream is energy as much as it is anything else, a grasp on everything you want to happen—or not happen.

Establishing goals is all right if you don't let them deprive you of interesting detours.
—Doug Larson

Instructions for Visioning

— **Go to some favorite place of yours,** preferably in some natural setting where you are alone and not pressured by other responsibilities, time constraints, or phone calls. Relax and allow your mind to see how you want your next chapter to come out in all its important respects—your personal life, your important activities, the people you are connected to, and anything else of great importance in your life at this time.

— **Give yourself permission to dream** without censoring yourself around money or time or gender issues. Simply imagine your preferred future, with you at your best. Ask yourself questions like these:

~ Where will I be geographically?

~ Who will be with me?

~ What will I be about? What will be important for me, providing meaning and happiness and security?

~ How will I be at work? Home? Play? Travel? Creative activities?

— **Let your vision touch everything you want trans-**

formed. Make it a central dream that informs all of your life. Review it over and over until the same vision or dream keeps repeating itself, to your continued delight. Then get your notebook or journal and write down every detail and aspect of your dream.

— **Write out your vision or dream for the next chapter of your life as a story or drama unfolding.** Let it have elegance and even grandiosity, so that you can relish its flavor and richness. Let it have the power to inspire, enrapture, and pull you into it during the next few years.

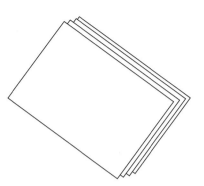

Step 3. *What Is Your Plan for the Next Chapter of Your Life?*

If purpose is the source of your deepest affirmations, and visioning is how you picture your optimal possibilities for the near future, planning is how you implement the vision in the real world, *now*.

~ Purpose is spiritual, value-based, and motivating, although often not immediately applicable. It is your "why."

~ Visioning is dreamy, pictorial, imaginative, soft-headed, energy releasing, and not literal. It is more definite than purpose but not yet directly applicable to daily living. It is your "what."

~ Planning is realistic, logical, hard headed, definite, factual, literal, and time-driven. It is your "how." When you plan, you take your purpose and dream and break it down into goals, objectives, action steps, and time lines. Planning is a step-by-step process for making the dream happen, with a little worldly savvy thrown in.

To create a future, the dream must become a plan, as the dreamer becomes a planner. Planning is more than a bunch of skills; it is an inner force, a felt competence, a strength within us. The planner pushes forward with logical steps, like choosing reliable stepping stones to cross a stream. Through strategic thinking, the planner embroiders the dreamer's vision in the complexity of the world, weaving together technical and human resources required to bring the life structure into reality. The possible dream becomes a probable plan.

A plan is a living document, not a stone etching. Frequent evaluation is required, along with adaptation to new resources and opportunities as they are discovered. Yet the basic plan will remain, as a vehicle for making the dream happen. Plans need to be definite, anchored carefully in a sequence of events and a committed life with time management.

First, conduct an inventory (below) of what activities you want to include in the next chapter of your life. Then plunge into the planning process and define your plan.

Planning Item: An Activities Inventory

Integrate the information you have obtained from this book by forming three sets of potential action steps for your future: what to hold on to, what to let go of, and what to take on. Make lists in your notebook or journal, with as many items as you want under each heading:

> *Buddha left a road map, Jesus left a road map, Krisna left a road map. But you still have to travel the road yourself.*
> —Stephen Levine

~ HOLD ON ~
Activities you want to do more of
~ LET GO ~
Activities you want to do less of, or stop doing altogether
~ TAKE ON ~
New activities you want to begin

Planning Item: Prepare Your Planning Cards

Get a pack of 3" x 5" index cards or post-its and create the grid below on as many cards as you will use for your plan. Each card will represent one goal or objective. Don't overwhelm yourself with too many cards. Seek to identify your most important, strategic steps ahead, and let them lead you—throughout the plan—to more cards. Use a heavy rubber band around them so you can carry them in your purse or briefcase and review them each week.

We call these cards "stepping stones" because each one represents a destination on your preferred path. Don't fill out the cards, yet. Just prepare them for making a plan, filling out your preferred "stepping stones" for the journey ahead. Here is the grid to use on one side of each card:

Completion date _____

PLANNING CARD

Stepping Stone
(Goal or Objective)

_____

Action Steps   Dates

1. _____

2. _____

3. _____

Now, Construct Your Plan, and Begin Your LifeLaunch in the Following Sequence

~ **Identify the stepping stones** that will lead you as surely as you know how from where you are toward your vision. Place one stepping stone goal or objective on each card, exhausting your sense of the results you want to obtain from your plan before you spend any time on action steps and time management issues.

~ **Identify a completion date for each stepping stone**—In the upper right hand corner of each card that you intend to use, indicate the deadline date when you want and expect this goal to be realized.

~ **Create three simple, challenging action steps** for each card—Under each goal list three action steps and

dates which you will take to realize each goal. Keep each step small and easy so you don't overwhelm yourself. Concentrate only on the first three action steps. When you complete a step, create a new one— 4, or 5, or 6, etc.—so you always have three action steps and their dates in front of you until you reach your goal by the completion date in the upper right hand corner. Use the back of the card, or new cards as needed.

~ **Organize your cards**—Spread them out on a table (or if you're using Post-Its put them on a wall), so you can see them as a whole. Then invent some organizing principle that works for you: chronologically, or by topics, or by your values, or by your systems and roles. After you've completed your planning cards to your initial satisfaction, organize them in various patterns (passions, roles, chronology, or other categories that make sense to you) until you are convinced that you have the stepping stones you need and want to empower your next chapter.

~ **Rehearse your plan**—Be sure that your ultimate plan is your story or script, not merely a bunch of busy activities. Rehearse your cards over and over until you can tell your story of the next year or two of your life and how you will live, work, and love. Let your plan fulfill your mission, and your mission lead to your dream/vision. Remember that rehearsing your plan until you are committed to it turns you into an anticipatory person, ready to make your future happen.

~ **Enter each "action step" into your time management system**—When your plan is congruent with your purpose, your vision, and your mission, enter each action step in your time management system, with evaluation points every three months. Put copies of your purpose, vision, and mission statements in your time management system, along with photographs and doodling and small art work that represent your next chapter in life. Turn your time management system into your life management system.

~ **Network to facilitate your future**—Find support for your new plan with friends, mentors, training groups, church, or other community resources. Do not try to make your plan happen all by yourself. Let others know your priorities and goals, and ask for their input and support. Carry your planning cards with you in your purse or briefcase so you can review them frequently, update them, and keep all action steps monitored through your time management system.

~ **Review your plan once a month** to see how well you are doing. Determine these days for each month, for the next year, and write them into your time management system. Go to a place where you can be alone, to reflect on the path you are taking. When you conduct a review of your plan feel free to change any stepping stone when you have a better one to take its place. Rip up cards that in reality no longer make sense, and write up new ones whenever you need them.

~ **Hire a consultant or coach**. You may want to have a personal consultant or coach with whom you can meet from time to time to help you stay on course with your plan. Ask someone you see as a mentor to you at this time in your life. Here is a list of some of questions to ponder openly in coaching sessions:

— Am I sustaining the commitment I need?

— Am I reaching my goals and objectives on the deadlines I identified?

— Do I have an adequate support system?

— Am I enjoying my plan?

— Am I value-driven and passionate?

— Am I managing my critical roles and systems effectively?

— Are there substantial changes in my plan to consider?

— Are there minor modifications in my plan to make?

~ **If you reach a plateau in your LifeLaunch,** you will probably experience reduced motivation and clarity in your chapter of life. If this occurs, it is a very good time to sharpen up your sense of purpose and your vision again, to feel the power of why you are doing what you are doing.

. . . .

~ **When your life chapter needs a total revision**, start at the beginning of the book and go through this again. Even though you will know the language and the steps for making a profound LifeLaunch, you will probably feel entirely different about the process because your priorities and concerns will have changed.

~ **When your life chapter finally gets stuck in the doldrums,** as they all do, remember what you learned from the renewal cycle, and either make major improvements in your plan and begin a renewed life structure, or make a decision to end your chapter to cocoon and find a new chapter to enter. You will know which path is the right one to follow, but don't wait until others make you follow an exit sign not to your choosing. Change before you get comfortable with your discomfort. Pull your own cord and grow a new future. Bon voyage!

CHAPTER 10

Staying Power
Eleven Ways to Stay Renewed

> ## SELF-RENEWING PEOPLE ARE
>
> ~ Value driven
> ~ Connected to the world
> ~ Needing solitude and quiet
> ~ Self-pacing
> ~ Revived by nature
> ~ Creative and playful
> ~ Adaptive to change
> ~ Committed to learn from down time
> ~ Always in training
> ~ Future-oriented
> ~ Personal leaders

Thousands of people have talent. The one and only thing that counts is: Do you have staying power?
—Noel Coward

Our lives are bombarded day after day by repetitive news stories, intrusive advertisements, demanding deadlines, and abundant options. Like blotters, we soak up more input than we want or need, and we often feel inundated and overwhelmed by the global flow that is consumer oriented—right at us. Our abundant options often lead to few real choices.

Unlike the past when the institutions around us filtered and monitored our input, today's "information" and "options" arrive from unending sources to each one of us—by television, radio, newspapers, mail, fax, electronic communication, magazines, books, and on and on.

Even if we have convincing life plans, and are leading fairly balanced and happy lives, we fall prey to flooding, overload, and stress. That's our environment. Winning work styles and lifestyles require continuous efforts at self-renewal, so our cups can always be at least half full. You need to invent a hundred and one ways to sustain your confidence, energy, and determination in the daily rush of things.

~ You can't rely on "off time" for renewal—weekends, vacations, special moments. Your primary need for renewal is within the daily flow of your life, in your ordinary time and space, not in the episodic "time outs" of weekends and holidays.

~ Think of renewal as a steady series of very simple actions you can tap into at moments throughout each day, no matter where you are, to sustain your esteem, priorities, and commitments.

~ Think of renewal as ways to filter out information and intrusions that don't belong to you, so you can remain vitally engaged with your dream/plan.

Here are eleven categories to guide you toward continuous renewal. Under each category are specific renewal ideas for you to consider. Select the ones that make sense to you, and build them into your LifeLaunch plan .

I am not bound to win, I am bound to be true. I am not bound to succeed, but I am bound to live up to the light I have.
—Abraham Lincoln.

1. Stay Value Driven

Self-renewing people know what they prefer. They are anchored within themselves and creatively bonded to persons they care about and projects they believe in. Something is always at stake because something matters, and time gets organized around those critical priorities.

These are the people who are wanted by the world to take on endless responsibilities—to serve on Boards, and assume schedules that may have little to do with their life plans and social commitments. To stay within the parameters of your passionate values at this time in your life, consider the following practical ideas for staying renewed and on course.

Some ways to practice renewal through value-driven behaviors:

~ Join or create a group of persons who share your values, a group that meets about every two weeks where members can talk about their life/work situations, feelings, and network needs.

~ Participate actively in a religious or other organization that reinforces and supports your basic beliefs, something you can attend and be connected to without having to take on leadership roles and ongoing responsibilities except when you want to.

~ When you think about people you care about, phone or write to them.

~ Thank people with handwritten notes.

~ Maintain boundaries between you and everyone else. Say yes and no clearly.

~ Each quarter of the year, meet and get to know one new person, and do something special to renew your ties with two old friends.

~ Let small presents to the special loves of your life become a familiar ritual.

~ Have a favorite charity, cause, or nonprofit organization that you support financially, and with volunteer time, and more.

2. Be Connected to the World about You

There is a strong tendency today for effective adults to become specialists in certain areas of their lives while neglecting the resources for renewal all around them. The truth is that the more you are engrossed by a career or family, the more you need to seek balance through other contacts. Adults who stay at their best throughout the many chapters of their lives put as much time into being effective generalists as they do into being effective specialists.

A generalist might have good friends outside of the speciality area, or belong to organizations—a spa, club, church, civic group—that deal with social connectedness. All of us have remarkable resources at our disposal,

For the most part, all the external side of life must be neglected; one should not bother about it. Do your own work.
—Tolstoy

if we choose to relate to them: libraries and book stores, public gardens and zoos, museums and art galleries, environmental activities, sports organizations, adventure clubs, and adult education classes. Through connections like these you nurture your basic humanity—the person inside—and deepen your roots in your community. Practice caring, and deliver whatever you promise. If you want to increase your connections to the world around you, consider these practical ways:

~ Spend about a month simply investigating the resources of your community. Check out the Chamber of Commerce, listings in the yellow pages under "associations" and "societies." In fact, study the yellow pages carefully to get an overview of what's going on in your community.

Imagine that you have just arrived in your present location, even if you have lived there for twenty years. Visit organizations and institutions you are not familiar with, gather brochures and information, and then ponder your needs and life opportunities within the broad spectrum of resources immediately available to you. Move toward membership or participation in the events you prefer.

~ Consider identifying certain activities as lifetime interests, so that you can connect to some sport, hobby, and cause in which you continue to grow throughout your entire life.

~ Perhaps you can enter into some of these areas with someone you care about—your spouse, close friend, or one of your children—so that your involvement has a secondary objective to enrich some relationship you value.

~ Connecting to the world can take you far away, too. The Pacific rim is well worth your considering, because of its presumed economic dominance in the twenty-first century. Learn a language from there, visit there and make friends with nationals who share your interests. Just get connected. The rest will follow.

Nature is beautiful,
simple and direct—
for her,
nothing is lacking
and nothing
is superfluous.
—Leonardo da Vinci

Come, my friends,
'Tis not too late to seek a
newer world.
Push off, and sitting well
in order smite
The sounding furrows;
for my purpose holds
To sail beyond the
sunset, and the baths
Of all the western stars,
until I die.
—Alfred Lord Tennyson

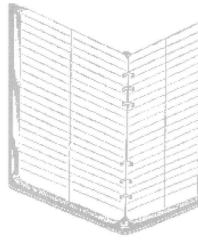

Removing oneself voluntarily from one's habitual environment promotes self-understanding and contact with those inner depths of being which elude one in the hurly-burly of day-to-day life.
—Anthony Storr

3. Find Time Each Day for Solitude and Quiet

Persons seeking to stay true to their purpose and vision tend to spend most of their lives being busy, particularly throughout the midlife years. For such people, renewal often comes from moments of solitude and quiet scattered across the days and weeks of active engagement. When you have time alone, be sure you are free of intruders such as phones, faxes, television, and radio. Here are some specific, practical suggestions:

~ Seek a private place where you won't be disturbed—a park, a small restaurant, a walk, a bathroom, an automobile. If possible, claim a room at home just for solitude and peace. Then figure out how you best listen to your inner self and beyond—through meditation, prayer, books of quotations, and silence.

~ Take a retreat alone once a year, at some facility where you are not known—a place that will leave you to your solitude. Concentrate on introspection, life review, taking stock, and recalibrating your priorities.

~ Use your commute time for quietness and solitude, if you are traveling alone. Leave the radio and tape recorder off, but feel free to talk to yourself if that stimulates inner talk. You might want to keep a pad and pen handy in case you get some ideas you want to remember, or you could have a small tape recorder on the seat next to you to record some of your key thoughts. Some people record their ideas on their way to work and listen to what they said on their way home so they can stay in tune with their inner space.

~ As often as you can, eat your lunch away from your work place, alone, in a quiet setting. Concentrate upon finding congruence between your inner thoughts and your work, and remember Thoreau's constant refrain: "Simplify, simplify."

~ Go to a church, chapel, synagogue, or mosque on a regular schedule each week to sit and meditate. Choose a setting that helps connect you to your roots and spiritual heritage. Engage in traditional as well as spontaneous prayers, and write down any special ideas that come to you. If you are not committed to a religious heritage, sit and meditate at a garden setting or some other place that has quiet beauty.

~ Have an "alone" chair somewhere in your home that you go to regularly, just to be by yourself, with nothing to do. If possible, get up very early in the morning and sit in this chair to contemplate the day ahead of you.

4. Pace Yourself

Self-renewing persons have a long term perspective on their lives, which translates into time management priorities and strategic steps. When they overextend themselves, they recognize the feelings, and step back to reflect on ways to get control of pacing and balance before they get overwhelmed or stressed. Some possible ways to pace yourself are these:

~ Each Friday, before you leave work for the weekend, review your week's schedule and *evaluate* how you did at pacing and balance. Then turn to your next week's schedule to see if you can make improvements in it before next Friday's review.

~ Identify someone you know and respect for his or her ability to control pacing and balance, and arrange to have lunch together once a month to talk about these issues. Put what you learn into immediate practice.

~ Take a sabbatical, at least once a decade, for whatever length of time you can afford and manage. This is a time-honored way to get back to basics with your life, and to clean out the superfluous activities. Go somewhere—alone if possible—without an agenda or plan. Spend your time imagining, wondering, and laughing a lot. When you come home your friends will think you must have taken an advanced course from a "master." You did!

God grant me the serenity to accept the things I cannot change, the courage to change the things I can, and the wisdom to know the difference.
—Reinhold Niebuhr

5. Have Contact with Nature as Often as You Can

Nature is a universal resource for renewal. Identify your favorite outdoor experiences and make regular arrangements on a weekly basis—walk a beach, a path in a park, or the sidewalks to and from work; listen to the wind, splashing water, the sounds of birds, or forest noises; feel the sun, rain, wind, or snow; talk to the sunrise and sunsets, the trees, and the flowers. The more you stay in vital dialogue with nature, the more you will feel energy and encouragement for everything you do.

~ Have lunch in a park.

~ Find a quiet place on your daily commute to stop for a quiet encounter with the sun, the breeze, and perhaps a singing bird.

~ During summers arrange for a weekly picnic at some beautiful location with friends and your families.

~ Plan one vacation a year around visiting the most beautiful places you can find. Waterfalls, National Parks, mountains, oceans, streams, lakes, the great plains, deserts.

Everything is connected to everything else. Everything must go somewhere. Nature knows best. There is no such thing as a free lunch.
—Barry Commoner

6. Be Creative and Playful

Give your inner child more freedom to be. Be spontaneous playful, and engaged in creative activities. Laugh, seek fun, feel free, sing, and discover more deep down vitality. If you're not having fun, you're not much fun to be around. Laughter and creativity are transcendent forces in our lives that permit us to see our own absurdity and limits. Give the world a break by tapping your inner energy just for the fun of it, without any other reason or purpose. In return you will feel light and childlike, and perhaps a little silly for awhile.

~ Go to settings where you can safely and freely express yourself, without worry or fear of embarrassment.

~ Plan creative activities that include playful roles—sports activities, volunteer work in a zoo or infant nursery, an art class, visit to a museum, early evening hike, or meeting with people more spontaneous and creative than you are (try a bunch of five-year-olds).

~ Take lessons for learning a musical instrument, voice, or dance.

~ Schedule regular meetings with some young person you know to see what you can learn about spontaneous expression, laughter, and fun. He or she may want to learn something from you in exchange.

~ At least once a month do something totally absurd.

Most of the time I don't have much fun, and the rest of the time I don't have any fun at all.
—Woody Allen

7. Adapt to Change

Self-renewing persons keep pursuing their best options, instead of staying stuck with yesterday's blessings. They know how to adapt to new perspectives, goals, and ways of thinking.

~ Be prepared to lose.

~ Remain definite but flexible.

~ Focus on making things qualitatively better, not quantitatively bigger.

~ Confront when necessary, admit your mistakes, and negotiate differences.

~ Maintain good friends who are much younger and much older than you.

~ Volunteer in a hospice or similar facility to work with people adapting to change at levels far beyond yours.

8. Learn from Down Times

Self-renewing people learn from their disappointments. Like all of us, their lives have times full of funk and discouragement. But they know they can ride through such times, because they've done it hundreds of times with success. They have a high tolerance for ambiguity and dissonance, and when they experience conflict, they move right into it, to resolve it as directly and as quickly as possible. They accept the loose ends and unfinished business of their lives as part of their own future agenda.

Change ever, too;
we have no home,
…But gathering,
as we stray, a sense
Of Life, so lovely
and intense,
It lingers when
we wander hence.
—John Masefield

People are like stained-glass windows. They sparkle and shine when the sun is out, but when the darkness sets in, their true beauty is revealed only if there is a light from within.
—Elisabeth Kubler-Ross

~ Yell in the car, when you're alone. Or, speak softly.

~ Recycle yourself before the world recycles you.

~ If your memory is slipping, write down what you need to remember, a day at a time.

~ Contemplate your death, and live today more fully.

~ Cultivate a friend who will listen to you when you feel funky, disappointed, or blue. Be sure to reverse roles whenever your friend needs to talk more than you do.

~ Don't expect life to be fair, but be as fair as you can be.

~ Never underestimate your power to resist change.

9. Always Be in Training

Self-renewing persons never stop learning. They know how to ask fundamental questions and pursue valid answers. They know how to live without answers when none are available. When learning, they feel drawn into the future, to new possibilities. Through training they find new dreams to explore. When they have absorbed enough information and knowledge, they concentrate upon wisdom and mastery—living the truth they know to be important. Because they love learning, they are often recognized as leaders.

~ Read selected magazines and books daily.

~ Write to yourself, in a journal. Notice your key words and significant phrases. Learn as you teach.

~ Watch only TV programs you have scheduled in advance; then turn the set off.

~ Master a computer and use it as an extension of your brain. Learn electronic networking and explore it frequently.

~ Take an interesting book with you, wherever you go, and you will find more time for reading.

~ Form a reading group with colleagues or friends, to read and discuss an essay, chapter or book, about once a month.

Expect nothing, be prepared for everything.
—Samurai saying

10. Lean into the Future

Self-renewing persons do not dishonor the past, but they love to ask dreamy questions about the future, like "what if?" And "why not?" They look for challenges that would deepen their experience and make a difference to the world around them. They rehearse various scenarios for how the future might be and choose the ones they believe in.

~ Don't use lack of money as your excuse for not living your dreams.

~ Live your enthusiasm.

~ Plan a day at a time, a week at a time, a month at a time, a year at a time, but always ahead.

~ Cultivate some friends whom you think are better connected to the future than you are, so you can have colleagues in this effort.

~ Rehearse small scenarios—a day, a week, a month— of your future each day, and the future will arrive more naturally to your liking.

~ Postpone anything but your future plans. If you're launching your life, you'll need to practice self-renewal without ceasing. Build it into your lifestyle, your work style, your home life. Before saying "I've just got to unwind," ask yourself, "What can I do to be more alive?" You will discover new ways to tap undiscovered sources of vitality, meaning, and hope. If you have staying power, you maximize your chances to stay in charge of your life, no matter what. Lean into the wind.

11. Develop the Leader Within You

Self-renewal eventually leads to self-transcendence. As you succeed as a person, you find new opportunities, resources, and leadership roles in the complex world around you. LifeLaunch is not truly an individual act. We plan as couples, families, work organizations, churches and civic groups, communities, governmental bodies, nations, and beyond. To sustain your personal plan and to feel empowered over time, you need to stay linked to

Where are the Jeffersons and Lincolns of today? The answer, I am convinced, is that they are among us. Out there in the settings with which we are all familiar are the unawakened leaders, feeling no overpowering call to lead and hardly aware of the potential within.… How do you send out a call to the unawakened leaders? How do you make them aware of their leadership potential? How do you make leadership feasible and tolerable for leaders?… It is my belief that with some imagination and social inventiveness we could tap these hidden reserves—not just for government, not just for business, but for all the diverse leadership needs of a dynamic society.
—John Gardner

150

From my point of view, it is immoral for a being not to make the most intensive effort every instant of his life.
—Ortega Y'Gasset

Atomizing, rugged individualism must be balanced by a renewal of commitment and community if they are not to end in self-destruction or turn into their opposites. Such a renewal is indeed a world waiting to be born if we only had the courage to see it.
—Robert Bellah

social activities and resources congruent with your plan. Personal hope languishes without reliable social institutions engaged in their own self-renewal.

Item: The world seems more fragile, temporary, and dangerous than it used to. The operative word here is "seems," and this is the only environment in which you have endless opportunities to make a difference.

Item: People seem cynical about the world, governments, and big business these days. Cynicism is a response we humans create when we are overwhelmed and intimidated by the enormity of the problems that now penetrate our minds daily. Cynicism links to negativism, passivity, moral insensitivity, and self-destruction. You have a choice. If you are successful at managing your life through LifeLaunch after LifeLaunch, you can't afford to be cynical. You have to be cautiously optimistic to trust in the future, to live your dream, and to manage your plans. This trust goes further than your plan.

Transcend your need for support in order to lend support to the maintenance of the world around you, as part of your plan, so it can reciprocate with stable resources for the fulfillment of your plan. Call it stewardship, caring, or just plain smart. You and I won't be working on personal excellence if our social milieu is a swamp.

Personal leadership is a natural outgrowth of people who succeed at life, and that takes different ones of us in different directions.

~ When you have a LifeLaunch that makes you cautiously optimistic about your future, you want to add something of value to the future beyond your plan.

~ When you have a deep and compelling sense of purpose, you want to link up with callings beyond your personal needs.

~ The older you get, the more you live by gratitude and appreciation, and are attracted to serving the institutions that link generation after generation.

There is a latent leadership potential of men and women in our society—immersed in careers and families, experienced in democratic process, and determined to leave the planet in better shape than they found it. These mature adults have already succeeded at much of life and are ready to address the human prospect in its twenty-first century settings where all of our LifeLaunches will soon occur.

The tides are in our veins, we still mirror the stars, life is your child, but there is in me Older and harder than life, and more impartial, the eye that watched before there was an ocean.
—Robinson Jeffers

"The real voyage of discovery consists not in seeing new landscapes, but in having new eyes."
—Marcel Proust

"Either we have hope within us or we don't: it is a dimension of the soul... Hope in this deep and powerful sense is an ability to work for something because it is good, not just because it stands a chance to succeed... It is also this hope, above all, which gives us the strength to live and continually to try new things, even in conditions that seem as hopeless as ours do here and now."
—Vlacav Havel

"If one advances confidently in the direction of his dreams, and endeavors to live the life which he has imagined, he will meet with a success unexpected in common hours."
—Henry David Thoreau

Section IV

Resources for a LifeLaunch

A Reading List for Embracing the Future

MIND-CHANGING BOOKS

Handy, Charles. **The Age of Paradox**. Cambridge: Harvard Business School Press, 1994. Building on his earlier book, **The Age of Unreason,** Handy writes about the paradoxes of our time and how we can find meaning and continuity in our lives.

Hillman, James. **Kinds of Power—A Guide to Its Intelligent Uses**. New York: Doubleday, 1995. A most intriguing excursion on real power and how to use it.

Kennedy, Paul. **Preparing for the Twenty-First Century**. New York: Random House, 1993. Everyone who is awake and caring should read this book and discuss it—before the year 2,000.

Kotter, John P. **The New Rules: How to Succeed in Today's Post-Corporate World**. New York: Free Press, 1995. A "must read" for those who really want to understand the multiple implications of globalism.

Langer, Ellen. **Mindfulness**. Reading, MA: Addison-Wesley, 1989. A different way to think about being conscious and awake.

Mandela, Nelson. **Long Walk to Freedom**. Boston: Little, Brown: 1994. The most significant autobiography of the 20th century. Please read it.

Myers, David G. **The Pursuit of Happiness—Who is Happy, and Why**. New York: Morrow, 1992. A solid opus on what happiness really is.

Whyte, David. **The Heart Aroused.** New York: Doubleday, 1994. A poet's touch to corporate awakenings. Original and moving.

LEADERSHIP

Bergquist, William. **The Postmodern Organization—Mastering the Art of Irreversible Change**. San Francisco: Jossey-Bass, 1995. A philosophical analysis of the corporate struggle with the world of change.

Boyett, Joseph H., and Conn, Henry P. **Workplace 2000: The Revolution Reshaping American Business**. New York: Plume, 1992. The best book I know for an overview of issues shaping the workplace in the 90s.

Gates, Bill. **The Road Ahead**. New York: Viking, 1996. A remarkable book about how Bill Gates views the future.

Herman, Stanley M. **A Force of Ones—Reclaiming Individual Power in a Time of Teams, Work Groups, and Other Crowds**. San Francisco: Jossey-Bass, 1994. Promotes ways to keep clear about your own strengths and priorities as the basis for how to connect with others.

Hyatt, Carole and Gottlieb, Linda. **When Smart People Fail**. Revised edition. New York: Penguin, 1993. A classic on the profiles of success and failure.

McNally, David. **Even Eagles Need a Push—Learning to Soar in a Changing World**. New York: Delacorte, 1990. A positive and optimistic guide to leadership development. Very simply written.

Nasher, F. Byron & Mehrtens, Susan E. **What's Really Going On?** Nasher, Inc., 10 S. Riverside Plaza, Chicago IL 60606, 312-845-5000. A neat executive summary of the buzz words and trends of the 90s.

Pauchant, Thierry & Associates. **In Search of Meaning—Managing Our Organizations, Communities and the Natural World**. San Francisco, 1995. An original definition of organizational existentialism, to reunite the real self with everything around it.

Weisbord, Marvin R. and Janoff, Sandra. **Future Search—An Action Guide to Finding Common Ground in Organizations & Communities**. San Francisco: Berratt-Koehler, 1995. A simple guide to profound change with large groups and systems.

CAREER DEVELOPMENT

Borchard, David, and Associates. **Your Career: Choices, Chances, Changes**. Fifth Edition. Dubuque, IA: Kendall/Hunt, 1992. The best career guide in print.

Bridges, William. **JobShift—How to Prosper in a Workplace without Jobs**. New York: St. Martins, 1995. A rousing proposal for working in a post-job world.

Fox, Matthew. **The Reinvention of Work**. New York: Harper Collins, 1994. A compassionate call for finding your "work" and then your funding mechanisms.

Hakim, Cliff. **We Are All Self-Employed— The New Social Contract for Working in a Changed World**. San Francisco: Berrett-Koehler, 1994. A simple and compelling treatise on self-responsible planning in the work world.

Needleman, Jacob. **Money and the Meaning of Life**. New York: Doubleday, 1994. A searching document seeking a balance between spiritual hunger and material need.

LIFECYCLE EMPOWERMENT

Bergquist, William H & Associates. **In Our Fifties—Voices of Men and Women Reinventing Their Lives**. San Francisco: Jossey-Bass, 1993. A view of the Fifties as an awakening.

Berman, Phillip L., Ed. **The Courage to Grow Old**. New York: Ballentine, 1989. Readings written by successful elders.

Bianchi, Eugene C. **Aging as a Spiritual Journey**. New York: Crossroad Publishing, 1987. An excellent reading on the evolution of spiritual consciousness throughout aging.

Booth, Wayne, **The Art of Growing Older**. New York: Poseidon, 1992. An outstanding collection of quotations.

Bradford, Lawrence J. and Raines, Claire. **Twenty-Something—Managing & Motivating Today's New Work Force**. New York: MasterMedia Limited, 1992. The best book I know of for understanding Generation X.

Csikszentmihalyi. **The Evolving Self—A Psychology for the Third Millennium**. New York: HarperPerrenial, 1993. A refreshing treatise on the role of consciousness in finding fulfillment throughout the life cycle.

Elgin, Duane. **Voluntary Simplicity**. Revised edition. New York: Morrow, 1993. How to keep your life streamlined and free.

Friedan, Betty. **The Fountain of Age**. New York: Simon & Schuster, 1993. A powerful treatise on positive aging.

Goleman, Daniel. **Emotional Intelligence**. New York: Bantam, 1995. A remarkable presentation of evidence on emotional growth and development as a central force in human and leadership development.

Hudson, Frederic M. **The Adult Years: Mastering the Art of Self-Renewal**. San Francisco: Jossey-Bass, 1991. A very popular book on change and continuity throughout the adult years.

Kegan, Robert. **In Over Our Heads—The Mental Demands of Modern Life**. Cambridge: Harvard, 1994. Kegan asks the right questions about the current predicament s for adult living, although his proposals are often rigid and related primarily to the narrow field of moral development.

Larue, Gerald A. **Gero-Ethics—A New Vision of Growing Old in America**. Buffalo: Prometheus, 1992. A technical book on changing disengagement through ageism and retirement into active roles for elders.

Lifton, Robert Jay. **The Protean Self—Human Reilience in an Age of Fragmentation**. New York: Basic Books, 1993. A magnificent treatise on how to thrive in our age of endless flow, written by one of the finest living scholars on adult life.

Murphy, John S. and Hudson, Frederic M. **The Joy of Old—A Guide to Successful Elderhood** Altadena, CA: Geode Press, 1995. A new approach on how to make the most of the last third of your life.

Nuland, Sherwin B. **How We Die—Reflections on Life's Final Chapter**. New York, 1995. This medical doctor provides detailed descriptions of the doors to death, and engages readers in thinking about this unthinkable final moment in life.

Tannen, Deborah. **You Just Don't Understand**. New York: Ballantine, 1990. A good first venture into how men and women enter conversations with different expectations and verbal strategies. Much better than "Men are from Mars."

MANAGING TRANSITIONS AND RENEWAL

Bridges, William. **Transitions**. Reading, Mass.: Addison-Wesley, 1980. A classic reader with literary references, all about the "gaps" we all have between the chapters of our lives.

Cameron, Julia. **The Artist's Way—A Course in Recovering Your Creative Self**. L. A.: Tarcher, 1992. One of the best books out on how to be creative and stay that way.

Culp, Stephanie. **Streamlining Your Life—A Plan for Uncomplicated Living**. Cinn.: Writers Digest, 1991. A neat set of suggestions for getting organized and staying that way.

Hudson, Frederic M. & McLean, Pamela. **LifeLaunch—A Passionate Guide to the Rest of Your Life**. Santa Barbara: Hudson Institute Press, 1995. Five Maps for guiding yourself into a future you deserve.

Latham, Aaron. **The Frozen Leopard**. New York: Touchstone, 1991. A story about the author's midlife burnout and his struggle to find himself, on a safari in Africa.

O'Neil, John R. **The Paradox of Success—When Winning at Work Means Losing at Life, A Book of Renewal for Leaders**. Los Angeles: Tarcher, 1993. A great book on the need for leaders to have a rich interiority.

Saltzman, Amy. **Downshifting—Reinventing Success on a Slower Track**. New York: Harper, 1991. A well-written treatise for workaholics experiencing burnout.

Wurman, R.S. **Information Anxiety**. New York: Bantam, 1990. Makes a convincing case that much of our restlessness is media-based.

MANAGING GRIEF AND LOSS

Tatelbaum, Judy. **The Courage to Grieve: Creative Living, Recovery, and Growth Through Grief**. New York: Harper & Row, 1980. There is nothing dated in this book. It's a masterpiece.

Viorst, Judith. **Necessary Losses**. New York: Simon & Schuster, 1986. Tough talk by a deep and caring writer.

MALE DEVELOPMENT

Levinson, Daniel. **The Seasons of a Man's Life**. New York: Knopf, 1978. Levinson, who died this year, left this book as his major contribution—on adult male life structures and transitions. His **Seasons of a Woman's Life** just appeared, same publisher, 1996.

Thompson, Keith, Ed. **To Be a Man: In Search of the Deep Masculine**. Los Angeles: Tarcher, 1991. A great little reader with many points of view.

FEMALE DEVELOPMENT

Bateson, Mary Catherine. **Composing a Life**. New York: Plume, 1990. A very nice look at the introspective reports by several women on how their lives were shaped.

Troll, Lillian E., et al. **Looking Ahead: A Woman's Guide to the Problems and Joys of Growing Older**. Englewood Cliffs, N. J.: Prentice-Hall, 1977. A little known gem on the trade-offs women can make in their elder years.

COUPLES DEVELOPMENT

Campbell, Susan M. **The Couple's Journey: Intimacy as a Path to Wholeness**. San Luis Obispo: Impact, 1987. Especially useful for defining the meaning of coupling in the second half of life.

Dym, Barry, and Glenn, Michael L. **Couples—Exploring and Understanding the Cycles of Intimate Relationships**. San Francisco: Harper/Collins, 1993. The best new book on understanding coupling, it's phases of development, and how to grow within a couple's system.

Hendrix, Harville. **Getting the Love You Want: A Guide for Couples**. New York: Holt, 1988. I like this book and the exercises at the end.

Hendrix, Harville. **Keeping the Love You Find**. New York: Pocket Books, 1992.

Wheeler, Gordon and Backman, Stephanie, Eds. **On Intimate Ground—A Gestalt Approach to Working with Couples**. San Francisco: Jossey-Bass, 1994. New and powerful readings on how these therapists work to sustain intimacy in couples.

Wallerstein, Judith S. and Blakeslee, Sandra. **The Good Marriage—How and Why Love Lasts**. New York: Houghton Mifflin, 1995. A very grown-up look at how self-renewing people work hard to sustain self-renewing intimacy.

FAMILY DEVELOPMENT

Carter, Elizabeth A., and McGoldrick, Monica, Eds. **The Changing Family Life Cycle: A Framework for Family Therapy**. (2nd Edition) Boston, Mass.: Allyn & Bacon, 1990.

Galinsky, Ellen. **The Six Stages of Parenthood**. Reading, Mass.: Addison-Wesley, 1987. Very original and comprehensive.

Imber-Black, Evan & Roberts, Janine. **Rituals for Our Times—Celebrating, Healing, and Changing Our Lives and Our Relationships**. San Francisco: Harper/Collins, 1992. An original invitation to create rituals that tap the meaning of your changing life and relationships.

Josselson, Ruthellen. **The Space Between Us**. San Francisco: Jossey-Bass, 1992. An outstanding book on teaching interpersonal skills.

SOCIAL DEVELOPMENT

Edelman, Marian Wright. **The Measure of Our Success**. Boston: Beacon, 1992. A letter written to her children about what success really means in America today.

Etzioni, Amitai. **The Spirit of Community—The Reinvention of American Society**. New York: Touchstone, 1993. Promotes building a society on values and mutual sharing.

SPIRITUAL DEVELOPMENT

Ashe, Arthur. **Days of Grace**. New York: Knopf, 1993. A very profound statement of how one man of significant achievement sums up his life.

Carter, Stephen L. **Integrity**. New York: BasicBooks, 1996. Written by a law professor, this reads like a primer in moral philosophy. Blunt and clear.

Hopkins, Elaine & Associates. **Working with Groups on Spiritual Themes**. Duluth, MN: Whole Person Associates, 1995. Structured exercises for deepening spiritual awareness.

Roof, Wade Clark. **A Generation of Seekers—The Spiritual Journey of the Baby Boom Generation**. San Francisco: Harper/Collins, 1993. A scholarly examination of the meaning of spirituality in the boomer population.

The Hudson Institute of Santa Barbara

Seminars and Products

*Our mission is to facilitate visionary plans with adults
and their work organizations in today's open environment.
Our central goal is to train adults as masters of change rather than
its passive victims—to live their deeper dreams, and to stay in charge
of their lives, no matter what the circumstances.*

SEMINARS

1. THE LIFELAUNCH SEMINAR—This is the basic building block for all the Hudson Institute programs, where you learn the basic model of continuous renewal throughout your life. LifeLaunch is a four-day, residential seminar resulting in very clear life designs and deeply-felt renewal for the immediate years ahead—for persons, couples, and work groups. Over 15,000 persons have successfully completed this seminar since 1986. Conducted Thursday through Sunday several times a year, this acclaimed experience is conducted by Dr. Hudson and certified coaches of the Hudson Institute.

2. EXECUTIVE COUPLES RENEWAL—This seminar enables high-pressured, professional and executive couples to renew their bonds and vows, work through relationship impasses, formulate new plans, and discover new ways to affirm their separateness as well as their togetherness.

3. THE COACHING SEMINAR—A one-day seminar for learning the essential skills for facilitating adult lives and systems. This workshop will train you with specific competencies for facilitating, enabling, and renewing adult lives and settings. Phone, fax, or write for a current brochure.

4. PROFESSIONAL CERTIFICATION FOR ADULT COACHES—This eight-month, advanced program offers benchmark training for seasoned professionals in the new skill set of coaching, providing 12 days of residential, group and individual training, coupled with learning experiences in your geographic location. Designed for HR directors, OD consultants, career counselors, psychotherapists, and gerontologists, this state-of-the-art program uses a Coaching Manual and experiential training sessions, as participants learn to conduct assessments, perform as coaches, lead group process and make training presentations. We believe this is the finest training program available for learning professional coaching.

SPEAKING

Dr. Hudson, Dr. McLean and other members of the HI Team are frequent keynote speakers at conventions, conferences, and organizational meetings. Their message inspires people to take responsibility for the future, to become leaders, and to live their lives out of gratitude and stewardship.

COACHING & CONSULTATION

•The Hudson Institute coaches and consults with organizations around renewal and transition-management themes.

•We specialize in executive coaching, designing value-driven work systems, renewing downsized work systems and people being outplaced, and protirement planning.

•We provide in-house training in coaching skills, mentoring, leadership, and team-building.

Products

the hudson institute order form

I would like to order the following products:

Adult Years: Mastering the Art of Self-Renewal
$32.00/copy plus tax and shipping.
_____ copies

The Handbook of Coaching: A Resource Guide to
Effective Coaching of Individuals and Organizations
$50.00/copy plus tax and shipping.
_____ copies

LifeLaunch: A Passionate Guide to the Rest of Your Life
$21.95/copy plus tax and shipping.
Ask about discounts on bulk orders.
_____ copies

The Joy of Old: A Guide to Successful Elderhood
This book is remarkably "reader-friendly" and uses simple
language to help reframe aging as a unique developmental
opportunity with its own tasks, timetables and rewards.
$16.95/copy plus tax and shipping.
_____ copies

Discovery Guide: Provides a comprehensive set of
meaningful and reflective questions to assess one's current
life scenario and desired future state. Ideal for self
reflection or used in a coaching-client relationship.
$9.95/copy plus tax and shipping.
_____ copies

Planning Kit: Includes the LifeLaunch Book, a
deck of Planning on Purpose cards, Discovery
Guide and a set of Planning Card Post-It Notes
The combination of these four items creates the
possibility of an "at-home" planning session for
the next chapter in your life.
$34.95/kit plus tax and shipping.
Ask about discounts on bulk orders.
_____ kits

Planning on Purpose Card Deck
$9.95/kit plus tax and shipping.
Ask about discounts on bulk orders.
_____ decks

8.5" x 11" Laminated Map 1-6
$5.00/each or 20 for $3.50/each
plus tax and shipping.
_____ maps

Life Review: A Basic Tool for the Coach
$5.00/copy plus tax and shipping.
_____ copies

www.hudsoninstitute.com
350 South Hope Avenue
Santa Barbara, California 93105

EMAIL info@hudsoninstitute.com
PHONE 800.582.4401 | 805.682.3883
FAX 805.569.0025

Name _____
Company _____
Address _____
City _____ State _____ Zip _____
Phone No. _____
Amex/MC/VISA # _____ Exp. Date _____
How did you hear about The Hudon Institute? _____

Index